DESTINY AND KARMA
HAND IN HAND

PALLEVIKA DEVENDRA MEHTA

INDIA · SINGAPORE · MALAYSIA

ISBN
Hardcase 979-8-89519-535-2
Paperback 979-8-89446-672-9

Contents

Preface..5

Acknowledgement 7

PART 1

CHAPTER 1   Beginnings of a Timeless Love 11

CHAPTER 2   Whispered Confessions............................20

CHAPTER 3   The Gentle Touch of Teenage Love 32

CHAPTER 4   Matured Love at an Immature Age............45

CHAPTER 5   Long-Distance Relationship 52

CHAPTER 6   Confrontation and Crisis 61

CHAPTER 7   Is it the End of the Innocent Love Story......67

CHAPTER 8   Ego or Concern 71

CHAPTER 9   Coward or Altruistic................................76

CHAPTER 10   Love Never Gives Up 82

CHAPTER 11   Few Favouring Stars By Their Side............89

PART 2

CHAPTER 12   The Harder the Struggle, the More
Glorious the Triumph 97

CHAPTER 13   The News is....Good or Bad 106

CHAPTER 14   A Little Bit of Heaven in Our Arms 114

CHAPTER 15   Today's Moments are Tomorrow's
Memories.... 123

CHAPTER 16   Silence was Taken for Granted 130

CHAPTER 17   Suppression Leads to Frustration 135

PART 3

CHAPTER 18   Home Sweet Home 143

CHAPTER 19   In the Middle of Every Difficulty
Lies an Opportunity 150

CHAPTER 20   Blessings in Disguise 158

CHAPTER 21   Frenemy...172

CHAPTER 22   Silver Jubilee 189

CHAPTER 23   Pain and Pleasure.......................................199

CHAPTER 24   Ultimate Destiny Plays its Role.... 216

Epilogue *223*

Preface

Welcome to the journey of love, perseverance, and the incredible relationship between the two souls who have never given up on each other. This book celebrates Rahul and Mallvika's extraordinary love story, "Written in the Stars and Earned through Deeds." It spans over thirty years and is full of struggles, successes, and heart-warming moments.

Rahul and Mallvika are two totally different personalities whose love story began in the late 1980s as an adolescent relationship full of excitement and innocence of young love. But destiny had other plans, testing their dedication at every turn. Despite the obstacles and battles, their love grew with no restrictions.

A mature love story at the age of immaturity, against all, ifs and buts.....silence and sacrifice...... depression and disrespect ....drama and trauma....ego and stubbornness...yet winning them all with the sword of passion and patience....love and emotions...fortitude and travail...and most importantly trust and belief.

As you read the chapters, you'll see their undying dedication and the sacrifices they made for one another. You will sense their selfless love, joy, grief, and unwavering hopes tied with the "Threads of Fate and Echoes of Karma."

This story also delves into the lovely moments of their marriage, the joy and pride of becoming parents, the daily difficulties, and the retirement plans and their achievements. Rahul and Mallvika's story is more than romance; it's about developing together, supporting one another, and creating a life full of love and happiness.

It's about the ardent love that's ready to sacrifice oneself just with the intention of safeguarding their beloved.

The story is written by "Destiny's hands with guiding light of Karma."

Join us as we explore the lives of the couplets, who, in their own ways, had never given up on their love.

Acknowledgement

OHM SAI NAMAH

Thank you Sai for giving me a life partner like Rahul, such a lovable and caring person who gave me life full of love and affection.

I would like to acknowledge and thank on behalf of Rahul and me to all the wonderful people, our family members and friends who were part of our beautiful life. Your presence have brought us closer and made us value eachother. Your acts have built our trust and emotions towards eachother that strengthen our relationship. A big thank to our princess Neer who actually completed us. She was a reward from all mighty to us for all our good deeds. Our story clearly depicts that Neer was the solo reason for us to be born in this world, we were born to fulfill all her needs. Neer was, is and will always be our pride. A big thanks to all our family members, Voras and Tolias, our friends BONDS, not to miss our love messengers Rani bhabhi, Neepa, Deepak, Sona, Aashish, Saroj, Sejal, Malli ben without whom our long distance relationship would have not survived. A special thanks to all my rakhi brothers Ranish, Keyur, Veeraj, Naresh and Ketan who had safe guarded me and stood with me at the most difficult phase of my life.

Thankyou all for being part of our amazing life. We love you all.

Rahul & Mallu 

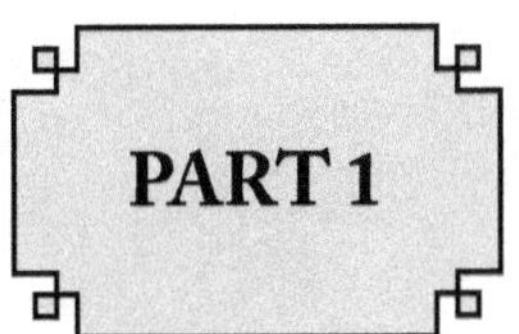

Was it you or was it me,

It was always blended to make it we.......

Was it won or was it lost

The lovebirds always fought for

Victory.....

CHAPTER 1

Beginnings of a Timeless Love

A sixteen-year-old boy named Rahul looked at the mirror and examined himself. He struggled hard to maintain his soft, silky, volumised hair, which kept falling on his forehead. Rahul sighed and reached to fix his glasses. The frames have been with him since he was five. Rahul was not what most people would call tall, dark, or handsome, but he was more than a mediocre-looking guy. He had a personality that could charm, a warmth that drew people to him like moths to a light.

Rahul always wondered if anyone would ever be able to see through the appearance and see the real person that was hiding beneath the surface. Even though he was not conventionally handsome, his quiet brilliance showed through his acts. His ability to plan things ahead of time caught people off guard.

Rahul was very shy, making it hard for him to connect with others. He was still a child at heart, enjoying the smallest things in his life. It seems like his innocence was a shield that kept him safe from the hard truths of life. He was a very caring person, always trying to keep others safe. He had a loving soul and a golden heart that beat with kindness and understanding. Rahul was always willing to help out, and his natural kindness showed in everything he did. Being kind was important to him.

He could never think of indulging in any kind of fight or argument with his close ones. Rahul, with this kind of nature, was usually misunderstood to be a coward. But on the contrary, he fought hard against those outsiders who tend to hurt any of his loved ones; in such cases, he turns out to be a very different person.

Rahul was religious, God-fearing, and believed in humanity. He strongly believed in "DESTINY "and always said," IF IT BELONGS TO US, IT WILL DEFINITELY COME TO US."

Rahul loved and respected his family, but FRIENDS WERE HIS LIFE. Rahul was the youngest member of the family, so his upbringing was a blend of coddling and subjugation. Rahul had a hard time standing out in his family as he was the youngest and had big age gaps between his brothers, so he hardly voiced out his feelings.

Chetan, his eldest brother, who was eleven years older than him, was like a father figure to him. He and the family often made the decisions on his behalf, thinking Rahul was too young to make the right decisions, which turned out Rahul to be a bit indecisive. He often felt like his brothers were the decision-makers, and he was not a part of it, being the youngest. This suppression behaviour often resulted in either silence or anger. But besides this, he believed and respected Ripun, his brother, who was five years older than him and always felt more secure with him. Rahul always believed and trusted that "Things would never go wrong with him, being Ripun by his side."

Rahul spends most of his time with his friends. He found comfort in simple things in life. He found happiness and peace in little things like spending hours sitting at the seashore listening to his favourite singer, "Kishore Kumar;" he enjoyed long drives, cricket, food, movies, and music…., but the favourite of all was "spending time with his friends."

"Rahul, are you ready? Have you packed all your stuff?" The silence had become thick like a heavy fog, but Chetan's words broke through the house; his words made Rahul's heart sink as it reminded him that he was about to leave the only house he had ever known.

"Yes, bhaiyla, all done," Rahul replied; his voice was a mix of sadness and excitement. Being away from the comfort settings of his childhood home wasn't easy, but the prospect of a new place and new environment gave him hope. There was a sign of excitement about moving to a new, bigger house, and also, soon, there would be an addition of a new member in the family, as they were looking for a bride for his elder brother Chetan.

Vinesh, Rahul's father, was helping Ranjula, Rahul's mother, in the last-minute packing. Ranjula, being the only female in the family, was always helped by the male members.

Just then, Ripun walked into the room, "Rahul, do you need any help?" Ripun was more like a caring brother to Rahul, and Rahul quite often took advantage and used to accompany Ripun and his gang, especially for movies.

Rahul replied," Ripun, I have packed all mine and our common stuff; nothing left."

"I'm Ready to move."

After the last few preparations were made, the house was filled with excitement. There was a neat stack of boxes by the door, ready to be put into the moving truck. Every item held a memory or a piece of their shared past, and they were all ready to move to their new home.

"Uff… mummy…please, let me peacefully watch Shahrukh Khan's serial Fauji." Mallvika got a bit disturbed and spoke to Jasumati, her mother, who was seated beside her on the five-seater sofa, irritating and pulling Mallvika's leg.

Jasumati looked at her in surprise and said," Mallu (her nickname), what do you like in this messy-looking boy? He is an average-looking guy."

Mallvika replies," Mummy, I don't know why, but there is something in him that attracts me; I love his messy hair falling all over his forehead; I like his cute, innocent face, even though he is not tall, dark, handsome, he has a spark in his eyes, and most of all the way he gives a look is so heart touching, and maybe this is the reason not only me, but most of the teenage girls are also crazy about him even though he is not a movie star." Mallvika continues," Mummy, I like simple-looking boys with hearts full of emotions, caring nature, and above all, who believe in equality, and definitely not a tall and handsome guy who feels superior, so you better choose one like Shahrukh for me." Mallvika hugged her mom and said with a mischievous smile.

Mallvika, at the age of fourteen, had very different dreams of her prince charming; she was never inspired by the image of "tall, dark handsome;" her desire was simple, cute, kind-hearted, and most importantly, "HEART FULL OF LOVE."

Brought up in a family full of boys, Mallvika often found it hard to share her thoughts, the only person to whom she confined in was her mother.

Mallvika carried a dual personality of inhibition and discretion. She was shy and suppressed in expressing herself, but when it came to her family and friends, she exhibited a different level of courage and boldness. Mallvika believed in God but never accepted blind beliefs. She always gained correct knowledge before accepting and following trends, rituals, customs, and cultures. She was highly inspired by her father, Suryakant, who believed in donating to mankind and had not practiced religious donation much. Mallvika, at a very young age, had gained expertise in all household work and management from her mother, Jasumati.

Mallvika was kind and humbled and always believed in helping and guiding others. She was a very jovial person and always kept smiling. She couldn't express or share her pain with anyone; in fact, since childhood, she had a habit of crying behind the doors. She couldn't hold on to sadness for a long time and would find a way out to smile even in pain.

Mallvika had a strong personality; she couldn't compromise on her self-respect, and this nature of hers kept her very choosy about how to behave and talk to others so that no one could disrespect her. She always double-checked herself before presenting anything she did. She was a headstrong girl and never backed out once committed.

Mallvika was a simple girl, away from all kinds of artificial beauty; yes, unlike other girls of her age, she never used any kind of cosmetics or beauty products; the only thing that fascinated her was nail paint.

As Mallvika and her mother were enjoying the friendly time, they suddenly heard loud noises outside. Mallvika peeped out from the window, 'Mummy, some new family is unloading their household stuff. Do you have any idea who they are?"

"Yes, they must be the Tolias; they are shifting to the flat above us; I spoke to them when they had come to finalize the flat; they looked like good people and are of our caste & community," Jasumati replied.

Jasumati greets Ranjula and has a short chat. Jasumati then invited them to come for hi-tea once the unloading was done. Ranjula happily agreed, saying how thankful she was for the warm welcome.

Unloading was done, and families met at Mallvika's house for hi-tea…..

Both families exchanged their thoughts and views on hi-tea. The moms talked a lot, getting to know each other, and they shared hobbies and experiences. Chetan and the Pappas, Vinesh Tolia, and Suryakant Vora, on the other hand, shared their views and expertise about business. Ripun quietly listened to the conversation, being part of it in between.

Being of the same age, Rahul and Kalpesh, Mallvika's elder brother, were talking more about cricket. Dhiraj, Mallvika's younger brother, as usual, was lost in his own world; he was quite mature enough at the age of twelve and always preferred to be in silent mode unless he was asked for something. The only one left out was Mallvika; as there were no girls, she kept herself busy serving.

Rahul, like every other teenage boy, had an image of her beloved, a slim, short girl with beautiful, straight, long hair and average looks. He always thought a pretty-looking girl could never choose a guy like him, but something strange was drawing his attention towards Mallvika. Rahul secretly glanced at Mallvika and found her so very different from his imagination, yet he was attracted to her beautiful, simple, elegant look. Her natural, curly, short hair made her face warm and attractive. She was not very slim and did not have the so-called perfect figure, but she had a curvaceous body with a good height. The natural glow on her face caught his eyes on her. She carried herself with a lot of grace, positivity, and sureness, which seemed to come from inside her. Yes, she was just opposite to his DREAM GIRL, yet Rahul was tugged towards her.

Rahul's interest wasn't limited to how she looked, but he admired her talent and excellence in the variety of tasty snacks she prepared, as the food was one of his weaknesses. Her excellence in management was very much evident from how she hosted at such a young age. Rahul couldn't understand the feelings, but he was stuck with her thoughts and couldn't divert himself; it looked like "love at first sight."

Mallvika was busy making tea and snacks; she couldn't resist but looked at Rahul whenever she got the chance. Her eyes were drawn to him because she found something familiar and connected about the way he looked. She soon realised and couldn't help but smile to herself as she thought about how much he looked just like the description she gave to her mother about her prince charming," the messy hair falling all over the forehead, cute innocent face, the spark in the eyes, the heart touching stare, the simple cute but impressive personality with a lot of humbleness visible on his face. There was no sign of superiority in his talk. Mallvika could feel the similarity but couldn't identify her feelings, and, without showing any more interest, soon got diverted; there was no sign of "love at first sight."

After the Tolia family had moved and set up, they were ready to relax and enjoy dinner. As they sat around the table, they discussed their happiness in finding good neighbours in the

Destiny and Karma: Hand in Hand

Vora family, who were also Gujaratis and shared the same religion, "Jainism."

Ranjula was deep in thought and couldn't help but think about how she longed for a girl when she was pregnant with her third child. She spoke about how upset she was that Rahul was born instead.

Vinesh, with a smile on his face, said, "Yes, I remember how disappointed you were. You started crying."

Ranjula said with a longing tone in her voice" how lucky the Vora family is to have a daughter, and that too like Mallvika, such a beautiful, talented and well-behaved girl."

Vinesh totally agreed and continued,

"Mallvika is like a princess; whoever marries her will be truly blessed."

Ranjula replied, "Yes, Mallvika seemed to have all the charm, grace, and beauty that I had once wished for, just like a beautiful plumpy princess."

Vinesh expressed Malvika's "plumpness "to be a sign of her family's prosperity. He said with pride," Khata pita ghar ni," it shows that she comes from a "healthy wealthy family."

Rahul, deep down, agreed with his parents. He thought Mallvika was the perfect combination of beauty, elegance, charm, grace, talent and kindness. Yes, Rahul was in love at first sight.

CHAPTER 2

Whispered Confessions

In a period of a few months, something truly special unfolded between the families. The approaching wedding of Chetan appeared to bind us all together like a magnet. The Vora family not only participated but also was right there with them, giving their all to every facet of the planning. It felt more like two families together than just a wedding.

Rahul and Kalpesh were soon part of this close-knit group that included a few other residents of our apartment. But for Rahul, nothing came close to the relationship he had with his school pals, the notorious "Honda Group," which included Naresh, who was very close to Rahul's heart, Keyur, Yusuf, Veeraj, Deepak, Raju, Ketan, and many more they got the gang name since they all owned a Hero Honda bike. Even after they moved away for college, their love and emotions kept them together.

And then there was Mallvika, who, despite their ten-year age difference, felt comfortable with the company of Chetan's wife, Reena.

Mallvika's heart, meanwhile, remained with her school friends, with whom she relished her newfound constricted independence. Their exploits brought them to beaches, movies, and last-minute get-togethers at each other's houses. It was a link created in the crucible of puberty, which got stronger with time.

We had happy and funny days because of the warmth of these ties. It seemed as though life had worked in concert to unite us all.

Over time, there was a quiet but strong change going on between Rahul and Mallvika. There was an obvious spark between them that they hadn't quite put their finger on yet. It was in the quick secret looks they gave each other.....the unconscious touch of their hands while passing by....... the moments of peace they stole while playing outdoors.....the accidental clash of their feet while playing indoors..... pulling Mallvika's hair ....to tousle Rahul's hair..... helping each other out with the wedding planning chaos and the most telling sign was sneaking support to each other in the group conversations. All these gestures came out intentionally from Rahul, although Mallvika was still not aware of her feelings and did it all unintentionally. Yet these signs got them closer and unknowingly built a path for their future.

Nothing was hidden from their friends, and they noticed and understood these gestures. There was a common factor in their friend list: Rahul's friend Deepak and Mallvika's friend Neepa were siblings. When Rahul's Honda gang got together at Deepak's house, they always talked about how

Rahul had totally fallen in love with Mallvika. Neepa used to portray this picture to Mallvika, and this daily routine had ignited the spark in Mallvika's heart, which was yet not fully flamed.

Rahul strongly started realising how he felt about Mallvika. He fell in love with her as she was beautiful, kind, caring, confident, and, most importantly, she was a happy person who spread happiness all around her. Liveliness was part of every meeting where Mallvika was present, and whenever Rahul was around Mallvika, he felt happy for no reason; above all, she made him feel alive in a way he had never felt alive before.

Mallvika, too, over time, started realising what she felt for Rahul but was not ready to accept. She was falling for him right from his messy look to the kind, caring, and beautiful soul he was. She appreciated the respect and equality he showed, especially towards females. He was exactly like the one she admired and wished for.

Their friends teased and encouraged Rahul and Mallvika, which made them feel even closer to each other. It was a dance of feelings that happened in the background but had a strong effect on everything they did.

The days went by, and the air seemed full of possibilities. Every moment was filled with excitement about what Rahul and Mallvika would face next. They were about to start a love story that would change their lives in ways they couldn't even imagine.

 Destiny and Karma: Hand in Hand

Even though they felt a strong attraction to each other, Rahul couldn't get rid of his fears. He asked himself over and over why a beautiful, confident girl like Mallvika would ever say yes to him; if Mallvika turned him down, they might never be friends again. It was too much for him to think about how this might hurt the relationship between their families, too.

Real love has a feeling of calm in it, a sense of peace that makes you feel liberated of any dependency, free of any need. When you really love someone, you go beyond their physical appearance, and you look deep into them, right into the core of their existence, their soul. And that's what happened between the two.

At the same time, Mallvika was torn between her growing feelings for Rahul and her awareness of her family's strong resistance to love marriages. She was afraid that moving forward with Rahul would mean going against what her family wanted, which she couldn't do. She knew that keeping her distance from Rahul was the only right way to keep everyone away from any future disagreements and conflicts, even though her heart was yearning for him.

The teasing from their friends made things even more difficult for them; it was like adding fuel to the fire; even though their friends were poking fun at Rahul and Mallvika, they didn't fully understand how hard things were for them on the inside. Their friends told them to follow their feelings, but they didn't know that family problems could get in the way.

It was a very hard choice for Rahul and Mallvika. These people were stuck between what they wanted and what society and their loved ones thought they should do. Every day seemed like a tug-of-war between their feelings, which sometimes brought them closer and sometimes pushed them farther apart. They were feeling confused between quitting and accepting.

As they walked this fine line between love and duty, they held onto the hope that one day, they would find a way to connect their hearts to the world around them. But for now, they were content with the bittersweet truth of what might have been; their love, which they had never spoken, was a quiet ache in their hearts.

DESTINY had its own plans. Even though Mallvika had made up her mind not to get into any commitments, she found herself caught up in the currents of love, just like a leaf is carried away by the soft breeze. It was like her heart had its own mind, giving in to her strong resolve as she fell more and more in love with Rahul.

Mallvika was going through a rough patch. She couldn't deny that Rahul had a strong hold on her. Every second that he was there, he was like a bright light in the dark, drawing her closer. She fought it hard, but she knew in her heart that she couldn't keep fighting.

                    Destiny and Karma: Hand in Hand

Rahul had been wrestling with his feelings for a while, but he finally made up his mind to tell Mallvika how he felt. "No matter what happens, I can't hold it in any longer. It's time for me to take a step forward, whatever the consequences. I just can't wait anymore," he resolved. With his heart set on confessing his love to Mallvika and explaining how she meant the world to him. Rahul asked Neepa to help arrange a meeting with her at a restaurant.

But Mallvika wasn't ready for that kind of meeting. That was something she knew she couldn't do because of how she felt. She really wanted to be with Rahul, but it was hard for her to stay away from him.

Mallvika tried to fight back at first, holding on to the promises she had made to herself so as not to disappoint her family. But love has a way of breaking down even the toughest walls, and she soon lost control as her feelings tore through her like a storm. She gave in to her heart's desires.

She finally made up her mind to meet him and tell him about what consequences would come and why she felt things wouldn't work out between them. She didn't want to, but she agreed to the meeting Rahul had set up.

Rahul was so very excited and nervous. Rahul couldn't wait to tell Mallvika how he felt; from the very first moment he saw her, he was attracted to her and how slowly and steadily she stole his heart. He messed with his hair as he was worried about how he looked, but soon got diverted as his mind was busy planning different ways to tell Mallvika how much he loved her.

Rahul got there early and was eagerly waiting for Mallvika to arrive. His heart was racing with excitement as he stared at the door. His heart skipped a beat as the door opened, and his eyes sparked as he could see Mallvika walking in. Mallvika was wearing a beautiful black cotton Anarkali with a printed black and red dupatta and not stuffed with any extra accessories other than an oxidised jhumka and bangles; she wore the usual black strapped watch on her right wrist. Her natural, beautiful face was glowing bright even though there was no sign of makeup other than the nail paint. Rahul couldn't take his eyes off her. Her wavy step cut hair bounced with every step she took towards him. She was wearing a lovely pair of black flat juttis, which complemented the Anarkali very well. She loved to wear high heels even though she was blessed with good height, but today, she chose flat footwear because high heels would make her look taller than Rahul, as there was only a difference of 3 inches between the two.

Mallvika was scared and tense right then. It was hard for her to figure out how to politely decline Rahul's offer without hurting him. Still, she couldn't get rid of the feeling that Rahul was special and exactly what she had been hoping for. Her heart skipped a beat when she saw Rahul in his stylish black and red chequered shirt and black jeans. His soft, volumised hair was all over his forehead. It was clear how humble he was, and the way he looked at Mallvika made her head spin. She told herself, "He's the one I've always dreamt of, but I can't believe he's here with the hope of acceptance, and I am here with the fear of denial." What does DESTINY have planned for us?"

Rahul's heart beat faster as Mallvika walked up to him. Even though he was shy, he fixed his eyes on her. Mallvika's presence was magnetic. As she approached the table, Rahul's nervousness melted away, replaced by calm determination. They greeted each other with a shy smile, the air between them charged with unspoken emotions. They sat down, and for quite a moment, there was a comfortable silence, each lost in their thoughts, gathering courage for the conversation ahead. There was silence in the room, but their eyes spoke volumes. Rahul got up the courage and said," Mallu, you very well know why we are here; by now, I am sure you also know what I feel for you. For the past two years, I have been secretly in love with you, and today. Finally, I plucked up the courage to say, he took a pause and continued with a shaky voice," I loved you since the day I saw you. My feelings for you have grown stronger every day. Mallu, I am a very shy person and hesitate a lot to get along, and this has always created doubts in my mind if anyone could really understand my silence, will someone understand the inner me, will someone make me feel worth it, and you do, yes Mallu you make me feel worthy, I have started loving myself. Your presence in my life has not only made me realise my love for you, but it has also taught me to love myself."

Mallvika got so emotional with every word expressed. Rahul's love for her made her feel on cloud nine, but the very thought of the pain she was about to cause him smashed her to the ground. Mallvika felt very hard to tell," Rahul.

We both know how we feel, but it won't be easy. My family won't accept us. Even though I feel like I should stay away, I am drawn to you. I don't know what fate has planned for us."

Rahul was shocked. He had no idea that things would turn this way. He was speechless and had a hard time getting himself together to answer. After a short pause, Rahul said, "I never meant to hurt anyone."

"I was sure everything would work out since our families live close together. That's why I got the nerve to invite you here." Rahul, after a pause, said, "Mallu, what makes you feel this way?" "Why do you think it won't work?"

Mallvika said in a soft voice," My family doesn't believe in love marriages." They are very clear about it. The elders of the family know the best, and they choose the groom or bride, and that's it. In light of this, I never meant to give you false hope. I tried really hard to stay away from this, but I gave up. I see now that I've also made things hard for you. I'm really sorry, Rahul."

Rahul replied, heartbroken," I could handle anything, but I could never bear to hurt someone for my own pleasure." Because our families know each other so well, I really thought there wouldn't be any problems, and that's why I let my feelings grow for so long. I love you very much, but I

                    Destiny and Karma: Hand in Hand

can't stand to see our families suffer. I'd rather go through it myself."

Mallvika nodded to show that she understood. "I agree with you. That's the reason I had to talk to you. What if things don't go as planned? I, too, hope that everything will be okay… But are we ready for the worst to happen?"

Rahul took a deep breath and then said, "I strongly believe that "WHAT IS MEANT FOR ME WILL COME TO ME." That could be why we're here today. Mallu, every parent wants the best for their children. In an arranged marriage, they look for a good family and a good groom for their daughters. Our families are so well-bound, and this is a sign that both families feel good about each other. And regarding the good groom, I promise to prove myself best in the upcoming years, and so Mallu, why don't we move on with a positive approach and hope for the best instead of the worst? I will do everything I can to make sure Suryakant masa (uncle) is happy about our relationship. I'm not going to hurt anyone in our family to be with you. I promise you and myself that."

Mallvika could sense the truth; she believed Rahul's explanation. Mallvika realised that both families share liking and respect for each other, so it should not be a problem, as Rahul had pointed out. But with all this, Mallvika had her own doubts; she said, "Rahul, I feel and hope you are right and believe for best to happen, but I am not a person who can step back if things don't work, and with this mindset, we both will be standing opposite each other, in case of disapproval from families. I am a strong KARMA believer; I don't give up once committed and work towards it, however hard and painful it may be.

"Mallu, it might seem like indifference, but I'll take any pain as long as it means our family won't suffer because of me," Rahul replied, his voice broken with fear.

Rahul and Mallvika made a choice together, but they did it in their own unique way. They didn't know what would happen, but one thing was certain: Rahul couldn't stand to hurt others, and Mallvika would stick to what she had promised.

Rahul then gave chocolates and a rose he had got for Mallvika. Mallvika instantly reacted and pulled Rahul's leg, saying," Rahul, I thought you knew I don't like chocolates; it's your favourite and not mine." Rahul replied," I very well know your likes and dislikes, and I am aware that you don't eat chocolate, but from now onwards, we will accept each other's likes and dislikes, and that's why I got both; my favourite chocolates and your favourite rose, and these things also have something more to say," Rahul explained further.

"Mallu, let's start our companionship with chocolates, which will always keep our relationship sweet, and the rose implies a forever fragrance in our life."

Even though their feelings were all over the place, there was still a feeling of dread. They knew it was against the rules to love each other and that the road ahead would be full of difficulties and problems. Moreover they didn't know what would happen, they couldn't help but feel a glimmer of hope, a belief that maybe, against all odds, their love would win.

They were lost in their thoughts as they sat there together in silence with their hands crossed. They only wanted to be together forever. At that very moment, they wished time would stop so they could enjoy being together and live in this moment FOREVER.

CHAPTER 3

The Gentle Touch of Teenage Love

Being in love is a beautiful feeling. The jitters, the butterflies, and the anxiety when you fall in love with someone is inexpressible.

The teenage love story began on a beautiful journey full of tender feelings. Everything was nice and beautiful, right from the emotional feelings, secret meetings, non-stop talking, long peaceful moments of silence, unblinking eye contact to the gentle touch, ruffling of hair, hugs, and forehead kisses. A single sight of your beloved fills your heart with joy, and one touch is enough to warm and tingle your body.

"I am excited to see Rahul all the time and feel elated when he is around. I feel intensely happy, "I am in love." My mind is full of Rahul's thoughts, and I can't stop talking about him with my friends. My heart goes pitter-patter when his name pops up in a gathering. I often take his side and sometimes even argue back in his defence, unconsciously, later I realise, my teenage love is making me crazy."

Rahul," Love makes me feel as if I can do anything. My approach to life is brighter and happier. It sparks a fire inside me that drives me to learn more about myself and allows me to grow. I have the courage to do things I didn't think I was able to do. Being in love makes me feel inspired. When I remember the limitless reserves of love I have within me, I become something else, something more than I am chasing. Love brings me back to a place where I find happiness, eternal peace, and enlightenment.

As the teens were growing up, the love between them was equally active. They often met on the terrace; they sat long on the staircase towards the terrace as there were hardly any visitors. They had lots and lots to talk about as to bridge the gap from their childhood memories to the present day.

The connection between the two gave them comfort that they could share their hobbies and skills, likes and dislikes, strengths and weaknesses, dreams, and passions. They communicated from the list of their friends to the first crush of their lives.

Coincidentally, a sweet custom grew between the two; Rahul gave signs to Mallvika whenever he left the house by smashing his door hard, which would be audible to Mallvika, so as to catch a glimpse of his sweetheart who used to wait either by her door or at her window, they captured the short sight of each other with an unsaid expression of wishing a "good day" ahead. On his way back, he honked his bike twice in a row as a clue for Mallvika, and Mallvika never missed peeking out from her window; they exchanged a smile with a question in their eye,

"How was the day?" And this was dedicatedly followed forever.

Rahul and Mallvika, like most of the teens of that era, were big fans of Bollywood. They expressed their love through playing romantic songs on high volume, making a cosy atmosphere that fit their feelings. Between the two, it was more like a questionnaire of selected songs that could express their feelings publicly.

The love birds went out for a movie, to a restaurant, and often to Naresh's residence. Naresh's family welcomed them with open arms as they believed Rahul and trusted his feelings. They were very supportive as they very well knew how serious Rahul and Mallvika were about their relationship.

It was time for their final exams, and there was just a month left before Mallvika could write her 12th boards and Rahul, his B.com second year. Both found it difficult to concentrate, but they inspired and pushed each other hard towards success. The day meetings were switched to late night meets. Rahul and his Honda gang usually did night studies at Deepak's house, but this time, the adda was moved to Rahul's residence. The reason was simple but deep: BREAK MEETS Yes, the lovebirds met at midnight, around 12 am to 2 am, and the new meeting place was Mallvika by her bedroom window and Rahul on the other side of the window as Mallvika's house was on the ground floor. They shared precious hours together, often just being together in silence, interlocking their fingers for long and sometimes a bit of conversation about their studies and future plans.

Finally, exams had started. Mallvika and Rahul both had followed an old tradition of visiting the temple for blessing and peace of mind before their exams. They were lucky as Kalpesh was not in town, so Mallvika's parents gave Rahul the job of taking Mallvika to the temple during his visit. It was an astonishing and blissful moment for both. Mallvika had been on Rahul's bike before, but all those rides were sneaky. This was a moment of delight and pleasure for the duos. Rahul felt so glad to take his lady to the temple with her family's consent.

As Rahul and Mallvika left behind their premises towards the temple, Rahul holds Mallvika's hand in his and kissed softly before resting it on his heart; Rahul then expressed his feelings," I feel an overwhelming sense of pride and gratitude to be completely yours, and simultaneously I feel fortunate and lucky that you are mine. I pray this journey has no destination as the journey with you literally means destination for me; I would love to travel holding your hands all through my life."

Mallvika turned pink as she couldn't control her blushing and just reacted by giving a cute hug. Interestingly, love had changed everything; the shy and silent Rahul had transformed into a naughty, expressive, romantic, confident guy, and the talkative, bold Mallvika was enjoying her new shyness, silent behaviour and more of a listener whenever Rahul was around.

Now that the exams were done, it was time for vacation and also time for the short-term detachment of the BELOVEDS. Yes, the first separation which was neither acceptable nor ignorable. Every year during vacation, Mallvika, with her mother and brothers, visited her paternal uncle in Ahmedabad. In fact, on the last vacation, Kalpesh forced and convinced Rahul to accompany him, but nothing similar happened now. It was only a matter of 15 days, but it sounded like a matter of age to the couple. Mallvika planned and tried hard to cancel the trip but failed and was left with no choice but to go.

Mallvika was standing by the door of her train compartment, enjoying the romantic hit songs of Mukesh, her favourite singer, played on her Walkman. The wind was strong as the train was moving at a high speed. Mallvika was enjoying the view of the rivers with full-fledged flowing water, which resulted in a cool breeze, which gave a bit of relaxation from the hot summer waves. She was gazing at the road with vehicles, looking like they were chasing the train, and

　　　　　Destiny and Karma: Hand in Hand

best of all, she was admiring the passing by fields that were fully ready for harvesting. The fields looked as though they were dancing to the tune played by the wind. She was enjoying every bit of it as she could feel the presence of her soulmate. Mallvika was in her dream world, which Kalpesh soon broke up.

Kalpesh, concerned, said, "Mallu, what have you been doing here for such a long time? It's so hot outside; you should get into the cool coach; if not, you will fall sick." Mallvika smiled and requested Kalpesh to join her as it was a beautiful sight to watch, irrespective of the warm waves. They stood for a while, and then Kalpesh said, "Now let's go in and play cards; we will come back when the sun goes down; it will be more pleasant and nicer.

Mallvika played cards for a while with her siblings, with all types of cheating and screaming, and it was great fun. It reminded her of how they all, including Rahul and other friends from the apartment, played cards at Mallvika's house. Mallvika said to herself," How I wish Rahul was here with us just the way he had accompanied us last year." Mallvika soon started missing Rahul. She got on the upper tier berth and began to pen down her feelings in the form of a letter, yes, her first love letter.

Mallvika had drafted every bit of her emotions on paper, she wondered how only in the span of 24 hours she was missing Rahul badly, How will she shell out 15 days, How she wished he could be with her now, how his company would have made this journey beautiful and remarkable….

Mallvika was so engrossed in writing letters, she had not realised, her family was there and they could doubt her for such unusual behaviour.

Jasumati, for quite some time, noticed all the changes Mallvika had been making.

Mallvika's glowing face, smiling for nothing, overflowing with happiness, and often looking distracted, had already created doubts in Jasumati 's mind, and today's act of writing a letter had stamped her doubts. Jasumati was smart enough to understand Mallvika's behaviour and soon guessed what was going on. Jasumati had decided to somehow read the letter Mallvika had just written to catch on to her behaviour. She was just waiting for a perfect opportunity to quietly grab the letter.

Soon, Jasumati got the chance to secretly read the letter; she read every bit of it. Every word written in the letter clearly expressed her deep love, but Mallvika had clearly hidden whom the letter was meant for by using different identities (names). Jasumati couldn't get to know to whom it was dedicated, but she had not given up and decided to secretly proceed on the hunt. Jasumati finally involved Kalpesh in her plan.

After a long span of 15 days, the love birds were going to catch up. Even though they had few chances to connect by telephone, they were impatiently waiting to see each other.

It was time for Mallvika and their family to arrive. Rahul walked back and forth on his balcony to capture the sight of his sweetheart. Soon, the wait was over; the red Maruti car pulled into the apartment and parked right below Rahul's balcony. Mallvika, who was equally eager to see Rahul, quickly stepped out and looked straight upward to the balcony, knowing Rahul would be waiting there for her. The clash of their sight was like raindrops in a desert, which was soon distracted by the family.

The love birds were eagerly waiting to meet; Mallvika was hunting for a chance to grab and finally succeeded. She pretended to be meeting one of her apartment friends and quietly made her way to where they usually met: the terrace staircase.

Rahul was desperately waiting for Mallvika as he just wanted to sit beside and stare at her indefinitely. Finally Mallvika was there, they hugged for a long time and sat closely. They had spoken about everything over the calls so they only wanted to be together and exchange uninterrupted staring. They were soon distracted by the sound of footwear approaching closer to them and at a jerk they set apart and waved goodbye.

Rahul was waiting for the colleges to reopen. He was too excited as Mallvika was done with her schooling, and now it was time for her to transfer from school to college. He wanted to take Mallvika for a long drive, and that was possible only by bunking college as it would give him ample time to spend together.

Malvika was trying to get admission to the college, which was very close to Rahul's college. She got her admission done with a few of her school friends; it was time for colleges to start.

★ ★ ★

It was a dark, cloudy day; everything looked so pleasant and nice; it was a perfect romantic day out. How could Rahul miss such a lovely opportunity, as he has been longing for it since the day he committed to Malvika? Rahul immediately planned to take Mallvika for a long drive. They were very thrilled about their first long drive, as until now, they had only been able to sneak away for a quick movie date.

Rahul picked Mallvika from her college and started for an unforgettable day out. As they drove, Rahul thought, "The weather was like a blessing from God, but the sight next to me was so ravishing that I hardly noticed the sight around me. This was also our first car drive together; I felt as though I was over the moon."

Rahul had prepared his favourite romantic playlist, especially for this drive; everything was so perfect: the music, the weather, and most of all, the fact that his beloved was sitting beside him.

Mallvika was too lost at the moment. The gentle breeze through the open window, the soft romantic music, and the presence of Rahul beside her made everything feel perfect. She glanced at Rahul, who was equally focused on her and the road and felt a wave of love wash over her. She felt so complete being with him.

They had travelled about 20 km from the city, had crossed the city traffic, and were heading towards the beach on the outskirts. The sight was so beautiful, the moment of the waves were so visible as the road was running parallel to the seashore. Rahul kept driving with one hand, and with the other, he held Mallvika's hand and gave a soft kiss on it; he continued his drive while holding her hand. Rahul was catching up with Mallvika's experience in the college; he was interested in knowing how Mallvika adjusted to the new surroundings, new environment, new place, new friends, new lifestyle, and new freedom.

They were both completely absorbed in Mallvika's lively talk and didn't realise the journey until they suddenly found themselves at their destination.

Rahul and Mallvika walked through the seashore; there was hardly anyone there; the only noise was the rhythmic crashing of the waves on the sand, which sounded like music played by the all-mighty above. It was a pleasure walking with the partner holding hands; the waves were chasing their feet, and the cool breeze added to the overall romantic environment.

Mallvika then broke the silence, "Rahul, I had spoken about everything I had in my mind; now it's your turn. What are your future plans as you get done with your graduation."

Rahul eagerly wanted to share all that he had in his mind; his voice was filled with energy," Mallu, I am so very excited about getting into my dream career "SHARE TRAINING." I'm anxiously waiting to complete my graduation, and in a real hurry to start working towards my career as I know I have very little time to prove myself, especially to your family, as they will start looking for a groom once you get in your final-year. The sooner I prove my abilities and achievements, the better are the chances for my acceptance."

Mallvika gets closer, rests her head on Rahul's shoulder, and continues to walk. Rahul continues, and the determination can be felt in his tone," Mallu, I've already started working on my trading skills and soon will get the neck of it. I'm not going to waste a second.

Rahul got emotional and with softness in his voice he continued, "I not only have to prove myself but need to earn sufficient to fulfil all your dreams and demands."

Mallvika interrupted in between,

"Rahul, I believe in your abilities, and I'm sure you will achieve everything you set your mind to." After a pause, Mallvika continued," Rahul, regarding my dreams and demands, I've only one dream, and that is to live a long life with you. I want us to be together in every stage of life where failures and success are part of it. No materialistic things matter to me. I have been definitely brought up like a princess, and everything I needed was given before

I could ask for; there was never a need to demand, so I really have not developed any demanding habits, and my needs were never bigger than the resources available, I have no urge for anything else. Yes, but one thing I will not compromise on is "YOU AND YOUR TIME." I can't get enough of it and will always be a bit more greedy than what I will get."

Rahul reacted with a cute smile and kissed Mallvika on her forehead.

Even though Jasumati and Kalpesh had their own doubts, they couldn't figure out anything much. Kalpesh frequently visited Ahmedabad as he wanted to get settled there. So, his hunt for the identity was at its peak.

It was time for NAVRATRI, the most awaited festival of Gujju's. Mallvika was a good dancer, and she loved to take part in RAS GARBA celebrations with all her heart. On the other hand, Rahul was very fond of it, but he was only a spectator; he couldn't get the grace and felt too shy to perform. During Navratri Mallvika, Kalpesh, Rahul, and his gang all visited and celebrated Ras garba collectively. Late at night, they used to visit the beaches and restaurants once the celebration was over; it was a proper gang out full of excitement and fun for all nine nights.

This year, it was a magical festival for the newly bonded couple; they were totally in a different zone even though they accompanied the gang. It was the best time of their life, the Navratri was never so entertaining, Rahul and Mallvika made valuable memories that they will never forget.

Jasumati and Kalpesh were actively chasing the person in Mallvika's life. Slowly, they started getting closer, but yet nothing was definite.

Kalpesh was in a bit hurry to know as it was time for him to move to Ahmedabad to his uncle Praveen's place for his future career, he felt like he needed to solve the puzzle right away. Finally Kalpesh with all the hints he had, tried getting things out from Mallvika's friend Rahida who was quite close to Kalpesh. Rahida got trapped and disclosed Mallvika's love for Rahul.

    Destiny and Karma: Hand in Hand

CHAPTER 4

Matured Love at an Immature Age

The duos had hardly enjoyed the most important period of their life and were caught within six months of their commitment. Mallvika's fears came true. The Vora family was shocked and disappointed; they had reacted exactly the same as what Mallvika had expressed; with Mallvika, they had no discussions, no arguments, no explanation; it was the straight verdict, and the verdict was NO, IT'S NOT ACCEPTABLE. However, the Vora family was very upset with the Tolia family and had one-to-one criticisms of them.

The Tolia family on the other end were a bit composed, their worry was the young age as there is no surety on the decision made at this age. They had no problems with either the Vora family or Mallvika but yes they respected Vora family's decision and asked Rahul to back-off.

Everything was in standstill mode. Mallvika was regularly watched by the family, and this made it hard for Mallvika to meet Rahul. There was no sign of the future; the soulmates couldn't meet to decide what to do next. The bond between the two families totally broke.

The Vora family shifted to a new apartment. They believed distance would separate the two loving souls. Suryakant took charge and drove Mallvika to and from college.

Mallvika was deprived of meeting friends, going on outings, and making phone calls. Mallvika was, in real terms, "house arrested."

Mallvika finally took advantage of a chance to skip college and meet Rahul. They met to decide on what and how to proceed further. Rahul explained what was in his mind," Mallu, we have to go through this temporary separation. Everything depends on how I convince your family by providing me with the right candidate for you, and for this, I need time. As of now, I should not hope for them to accept me as I have no identity, and we need to buy time by making them believe that we agree to whatever they say or decide for us."

Mallvika, in disagreement, interrupts, "Rahul, time buying means lying to our families, and I don't think that's right. I was already living in guilt regarding hiding our relationship, and now lying, my conscience doesn't allow me to do so."

Rahul further explains, "Mallu, I totally agree with you, but we don't have the right age; we are too young to take any responsibility, you are just 17, and legally, we can't take any steps toward our relationship. Further, I want to convince our families to start our journey with their blessings and to convince them we need time. So we have to agree to whatever they say for another two years for things to go steady, but if we revolt, they may take extreme steps and could also get you married early. So let's quietly listen to them, and I will work hard towards their approval, but as promised, I will never ever hurt them for us being together. You need to believe me and trust our DESTINY; it has brought us together not for "separation" but only for "forever togetherness."

Mallvika, with no other choice, had to accept the fact, "Rahul, I take your point and agree to every word you spoke, and I am also ready for time buying but if things don't work as we think, I will never agree for any further separation, I can't imagine life without you, you and your love has become my weakness."

Rahul held Mallvika's hand and looked straight in her eyes, than with much confident and lovable tone said," Mallu you and your love is my strength and we will get through this storm."

It's been three months since Rahul and Mallvika convinced their parents about their break-up.

The Vora family had moved to another house in the hope that distance would have no chance of their reunion.

Rahul and Mallvika were going through a very tough time. They had hardly experienced their partnership era and were uncoupled. Mallvika's migration to another location had deprived the duos from having a rare glimpse, and the conversation over the phone call was impossible as all the members of the families had struck their eyes on them. The only regular mode of communication were letters which were exchanged through a few common friends.

Rahul and Mallvika were very cautious; they were not ready to take any chance of getting caught, as this time, it would be out of the question to convince the families.

Rahal was busy with his final-year studies and extracurricular activities. He was leading his college cultural event, and one of his responsibilities included inviting all the other colleges in the city, which also included Mallvika's college. The couplets were happy thinking they will at least catch sight of each other, even though it will be for a fraction of seconds.

Mallvika had hardly enjoyed her college life, as things changed once the family learned about her relationship with Rahul. She was not interested in doing anything; she became more of a quiet person both at home and in college. Everything was at a standstill mode.

After a long time today Mallvika was interested in her outfit and accessories and how she looked, as it was the day when the duos are going to have a glance at each other after almost five months.

She was wearing a black churidar suit with a black abstract printed short jacket paired up with a black chiffon dupatta;

added to it, she wore a pair of black flat cut shoes, her regular black strapped watch, big black hoops, and a hair band to keep intact of her curly step cut hair. As usual, there was no sign of makeup other than her nail paint. The monochromatic combination was timeless and elegant.

It was time for Rahul to visit Mallvika's college, and as decided, Rahul was there during the break. Mallvika was eagerly waiting for Rahul by the principal's room, marching right and left; the excitement was at its peak. Capturing just a sight of the beloved was so very precious it was like "drowning man will clutch at straws."

The waiting period was over. Mallvika could see Rahul coming, paired up in his white pants with a white shirt and a navy blue tie; added to it; he wore a black belt, black shoes, and a black strapped watch; it was a clean, sophisticated look. Mallvika's movements were stock-still, but her eyes followed. Rahul, as he walked towards her, she couldn't afford to lose even a single moment.

On the other end, Rahul's actions were identical; as soon as Rahul entered the college, his eyes hunted for his beloved, and the hunt was momentary; he could see Mallvika far but right at his eye level. Rahul, even though he was at a distance, could notice Mallvika's glow and the beautiful smile on her face, which came directly from her soul.

Rahul couldn't take his eyes off her, but as he came closer, he diverted his sight. Rahul had gotten a rose and the chocolates for Mallvika, which were hidden under the invite. It was a big challenge for Rahul to give the rose and the chocolates without getting noticed. But he just followed what he had pre-planned; the moment Rahul was next to Mallvika, he accidentally tripped and quickly gave the rose and the chocolates to his sweetheart and softly buzzed "Love you, Mallu," in her ears. He immediately got up and moved ahead, saying sorry, as he was very well aware that he was representing his college and shouldn't be caught in any inappropriate act. He was happy with what he could capture in that short moment; it was enough for him to get through the exile period.

Mallvika was astounded but swiftly she veiled the rose and the chocolates under her dupatta, she was trying to recall what just happened, it was totally unexpected from a shy guy like Rahul, she was totally amazed and just a small gesture of Rahul had made her day.

Mallvika was exceptionally missing Rahul and was desperate to talk to him. She found herself lucky; she could grab a chance to call Rahul as her mummy, Jasumati, was occupied with the guest at home. Mallvika called Rahul, but Chetan picked up the call; Mallvika couldn't recognise him as they sounded so similar, especially over the phone. Chetan also took advantage and spoke to Mallvika, representing him to be Rahul. After the conversation, Chetan called uncle Suryakant and informed him, and he also warned him by saying," Masa (uncle), we have control over Rahul, and it's time for you to control your daughter, as we will not be able to take any more criticism."

Oh my God, poor couplets were once again caught and had to get ready for the upcoming storm.

CHAPTER 5

Long-Distance Relationship

All the measures to separate the duos were already taken, like relocation and Mallvika's house arrest, but the couple was intact; nothing could break them apart. Uncle Praveen was very frustrated and had decided to bring Mallvika to Ahmedabad for her further studies and he was also very clear about his thoughts of looking for a groom and getting Mallvika married while she was studying. Suryakant agreed to send Mallvika but waited for her first year to get over.

Tolias also didn't miss to show their resentment. Chetan spoke to Rahul," Rahul, you know very well we have no issues regarding you getting married to Mallvika, but not against Vora's wish. By now, you know very well they will never agree to it. Do you want to do something which will ruin the reputation of both families?"

But Rahul had decided to take a chance and talk to uncle Suryakant, he then replied to Chetan," we are not selfish and have no plan of getting married against anyone's wish, but will definitely talk to Suryakant masa and try to convince him."

Rahul had a long discussion and argument and was forced to promise a break-up, but this time, Rahul had not made any such promises instead he conveyed his thoughts very clearly to his family," I just want to say one thing, if I get married than it has to be only to Mallvika, if not I will stay single for rest of my life" and left the room.

Rahul and Mallvika had completed a span of 365 days; yes, it was their first anniversary. Both were desperate to meet, but the recent storm blocked all the paths of their connection, leaving no hope of meeting. Rahul had got a beautiful dress for Mallvika and passed it with all-time favourite roses and chocolates to her through their common friends. A lot had gone through the year, but even after the heavy storm, their boat had not sunk. The twosome can only wait and pray for their oneness.

It was time for the exam. Rahul was impatiently waiting for it so he could get started with his career. Rahul's mind was totally occupied with the passion of proving himself.

Mallvika couldn't concentrate well as she was depressed with things happening in her life. She was not only departed from the "love of her life," but she was deprived of all the independence she had; neither was she allowed to go out with friends nor were friends allowed to come home. The only place she got some de-stressing experience was in her college.

The exams were done, and without wasting any time, Rahul joined a share trading firm as a sub-broker. He soon got hands-on experience, and within a short period, he started showing growth.

Mallvika was also done with her exams, and things were going to be different for her as she had to move to her uncle Praveen's place for further studies. There were a bunch of fears she was fighting within. The long-distance will grab the limited source of communication, the rare glimpse of Rahul, and above all, the doubts that if the family really gets her married, in such a case, she will have no source of help. But with all these insecurities, she was left with no option but to follow it.

Rahul, too, was going through depression. He felt guilty thinking about Mallvika, as he knew she would be all alone there with no friends and family by her side, even though Kalpesh and her cousins, Inesh and Nimesh, would take care of her, but things would be different this time. Rahul was working hard to give Mallvika some type of comfort in Ahmedabad.

Rahul gave the address and contact number of Naresh's cousin Malli, who lives in Ahmedabad, so Mallvika has company and can also communicate with Rahul through her; moreover, in case of an emergency, she can seek help from her. This one source had given an ample amount of peace to the duos.

Rahul was working day and night, he hardly took any break, even if he was not working he avoided going out. His friends used to force him but he thought about how Mallvika was going through the pain because of him and always felt blameworthy about it. But as the saying goes "a friend in need is a friend indeed," Rahul's friends had been with him in his ups and downs. They were the reason behind the few moments of happiness in this span of darkness.

Mallvika got into a college in Ahmedabad. Mallvika was not interested in mingling, and so hardly showed any interest in college life, still there were few people who got connected with her.

Mallvika once went to meet Malli and felt comfortable with the family; soon, she collected a letter received from Rahul at Malli's address, and once again, they could connect through letters. Mallvika was going through a very bad phase, and her depression was turning to obsessive behaviour; she, out of the pain of separation, had engraved Rahul's name on her hand with knife cuts and wrote a letter to Rahul with her blood. Rahul couldn't take this; he, with love and anger, convinced Mallvika not to repeat such behaviour in the future.

Mallvika found comfort with Sejal, who was her old friend from the society they lived in. Sejal was aware of her relationship with Rahul. Mallvika was spending more time with Sejal; they went for daily evening walks and used to spend time at each other's place. The Vora family had no objection, as they knew Sejal well, and being in Ahmedabad, they had no other reason to doubt Mallvika.

Mallvika was missing her family, especially her mummy. Kalpesh and Inesh, being elder brothers, took care of her, and Nimesh always gave her good company. Mallvika's aunt and grandmother were also very humble to her.

Within sometime things were getting better. Soon Mallvika got a chance to call Rahul through a PCO booth, and it soon became a daily habit. Now the couplets were happy and felt safe as they could connect daily and update every detail that took place in their lives.

Things were again getting back to normal; Rahul also started hanging out with his friends as he could sense the amount of happiness Mallvika was experiencing.

Rahul had faced a few ups and downs in his business, but with his experience, he not only managed to get through the problems but also grew financially stable. He felt that soon, he would be in a position where he would be accepted.

For some time, the Tolia family was finding a match for Ripun, and soon they found a perfect match for him. Ripun's engagement with Riddhi was finalised in Rajkot (near Ahmedabad), and it was time for the family to visit Rajkot. All the members of the Tolia family except Rahul had arrived four days earlier. Rahul was not very interested in meeting everyone and just wanted to attend the engagement for Ripun's sake, so he was only coming up for a day for the engagement. Instead, he had planned a day for Mallvika. Yes, Rahul was first coming to Ahmedabad, spending a day with his beloved, and then going to Rajkot.

The most anticipated day had come, Rahul was in Ahmedabad. Mallvika and Rahul were exhilarated, they were going to meet after a long span of seven months. Rahul was waiting for Mallvika at the coffee shop of the hotel he had checked in, Mallvika had just arrived and reached the coffee shop.

As Rahul and Mallvika met, they lost all sense of being in a public place and gave a long tight hug, they were totally mesmerised. The bittersweet tears were rolling down with no sign of cease. It really took long and hard for them to release themselves from the most awaited hug.

Rahul just realised Mallvika was wearing a saree for him. She looked ravishing and stunning. Rahul was astounded and frozen. He then ecstatically said," Mallu, a sight of yours has healed all my depression and anxiety moments and has also boosted positivity until our next meet." He then gave the chocolates and the bouquet of roses to his beloved.

Mallvika with a smile sat on the chair, Rahul too sat across. Rahul and Mallvika spoke about everything that they missed in their regular calls. They were happy about how they could survive the long-distance relationship and also promised to have a better approach towards the upcoming period, as they yet have to face this for approx. a year more.

"Rahul, we could survive only because we could regularly talk, share thoughts and feelings openly, and listen to each other's needs."

Rahul agreed to it and added," Mallu planning visit was a bonus, and this time spent together will be like fuel to pass through the upcoming separation period. We also have a clear idea of the future of our relationship which has also helped us to be together."

Mallvika nodded and continued," Including and sharing our daily life with each other through letters, calls, and photos made us feel closer, even though we were miles apart."

The conversation was on and the love gestures too were part of the conversations. In between Rahul and Mallvika were getting naughty and had experienced the little physical intimacy moments possible in a public place. The twosome had hardly got time together in their courtship but one moment of being together was enough for the duos.

They had spent a beautiful day together, and it was time for them to say goodbye, with no hopes of any such meeting in the near future.

Mallvika's migration to Ahmedabad had not only depressed Rahul, but her mother, Jasumati, too, was going through a bad phase. First, Kalpesh had shifted to Ahmedabad, then Dhiraj had left for his studies, and now Mallvika, Jasumati was depressed, and her health was declining day by day. Finally, Suryakant decided to bring Mallvika back to Madras, as they were now fully convinced about Mallvika's break-up.

The Vora family had influence in the college, so on their request, it was agreed to study from home, and Mallvika was required to attend college only during exams.

Mallvika was back in Madras after her second year; she cursed herself for Jasumati's health issues, but she took good care of her, and soon Jasumati was recovering.

Mallvika realised that in the past two years, things had been difficult for everyone, and in all this mess, she missed the bond with her mother and wanted to compensate for it.

Everything was going well; the Tolia family was busy preparing for Ripun's wedding. Rahul was not very involved in any of the family matters; he had distanced himself since Chetan had informed Suryakant about the phone call. He only participated when it was necessary.

Rahul was doing good in his business with in between mishaps that every business faces.

The long-distance relationship between the twosome was at its best. It was six months since they last met in Ahmedabad, but the sight of the beloved in their eyes was so very new and fresh, as though they had just met. The daily phone calls were, most of the time, verbally silent as the heartbeats were doing almost all the conversation, and "WHAT ELSE" was the most common word exchanged between the two.

Even though the love birds were physically apart, they never felt the distance as they were always in each other's hearts and minds. All was going well, and it was an indication that good days were ahead.

CHAPTER 6

Confrontation and Crisis

How was that possible, the happiness in the couple's life indicated the upcoming storm. The duo's story was more of storm than peace. Mallvika was in her final-year and the Vora family specially uncle Praveen had buckled up tight towards the groom hunt. The family had already shortlisted a few from the alliance that had come for Mallvika; now it was time to see them and finalise the best.

Mallvika was totally unaware of this, as she thought her break-up story had fully convinced the family and they would wait till her final results. Soon, the news had dropped in Mallvika's ears, but by now, Mallvika had learned to face any tight situation. She was a bit scared but was ready for the upcoming challenge.

Mallvika and Rahul had to think of a strategy, where the boy and his family stands to reject Mallvika and doing so she will be safe and no question will be asked. The duos, by now, had become experts and had learned to be ready with plan A and plan B. In case plan A fails, they have a backup.

Plan A was to give inappropriate answers and show rude behaviour, which would lead to rejection and Plan B was to be implemented if the family was still interested, in such a case, Mallvika will reveal her relationship with Rahul to the candidate.

There were few meetings done in Ahmedabad and Mallvika succeeded with rejection, as per her plan A. There were few rejections by the Vora family too. No alliance was approved, so now it was their turn to visit Mumbai.

It was also time for Mallvika's final exams, and so Vora's family decided to visit Mumbai after her exams.

Mallvika was a little shaken up by the Mumbai visit. Mumbai was a new, unfamiliar place for her, where managing on her own would be almost impossible. Whereas in Ahmedabad she had Malli and was a familiar place too. Above all, in Mumbai there will be no possibility of any type of conversation between the twosome.

A few meetings in Mumbai went as per plan A. Now, it was time to meet the alliance, which topped the list shortlisted by Vora's; the family was very well-reputed and very wealthy; they had a great name and value in society.

The grandparents, parents, and three sons completed the family. The alliance was for the eldest son, "Pratish." Mallvika was

Destiny and Karma: Hand in Hand

instructed to wear a saree as the grandparents were also part of the meeting. The meeting was fixed at Pratish's residence.

Mallvika and their family had arrived on time. They were given a warm welcome, and the family, especially Pratish, was introduced to the Vora family. Uncle Praveen admires his personality; Pratish is a tall, dark, handsome guy. The normal conversation was between the two families; Pratish was also very much part of it. Suryakant felt his conversations were impressive, which pointed out his updated knowledge and confidence.

Whenever Pratish got a chance, he caught sight of Mallvika. Pratish then took Mallvika to look around the lavishly designed five-bedroom flat, and finally, they sat on the balcony to get to know each other. Pratish started the conversation by asking general questions about education, hobbies, etc. He then waited for Mallvika to say something, but Mallvika showed no interest in asking or replying. Pratish then asked a few more questions, such as, "What are her thoughts about joint family, wearing sarees, religious beliefs?" and so on. Mallvika had observed the family values and very well understood the joint family bond and the religious beliefs they had. So considering that she had replied," I don't feel much comfortable in joint families, I feel religious beliefs are blind beliefs, and I don't like wearing sarees and usually don't wear, but today my parents had specifically told me to."

Mallvika had not missed any chance of showing her negatively towards Pratish in the hope of rejection. Pratish could feel the apathetic behaviour, but something drew Pratish towards her. He liked Mallvika even though her replies were not acceptable.

The meeting was done, and the Vora family left. Mallvika was very happy as she was confident about the rejection. On the other end, Vora's family was very happy and satisfied with Pratish and the family; they hoped for a positive response.

An hour later, there was a call from Pratish's family; Mallvika praised herself for the way she responded, as she was so sure the call was good news for her.

Suryakant was on the phone. He spoke for a while, and suddenly Mallvika could hear him saying, "Tamne pan khoob badhai" and "Congratulations to you too." She couldn't believe what was happening and desperately waited for the call to get over.

Finally, Suryakant disconnected the call and gave the good news to the family," Pratish and family have liked Mallvika and are happy to fix the alliance. The family has suggested getting the engagement done as soon as possible as they have no more queries or doubts. However, they wanted to know our opinion and asked if any more meetings were required from our side, especially if Mallvika had any queries.

Mallvika was totally astonished and shattered; she couldn't digest what had just happened. Now, as plan A failed, she was hoping for a meeting with Pratish so she could execute plan B.

The Vora family had their discussion and decided to go with the date suggested for the engagement. They felt no necessity to consult Mallvika, as everything was so good, and according to them, Mallvika was lucky to get such a good match.

Mallvika understood very well that she was losing the chance to implement plan B; she was clueless and couldn't think of what to do next.

As everyone was happy and convinced the date of engagement was fixed, the Vora family was arranging for the rest of the family members to attend the engagement.

Mallvika lost all hope and was in total shock; her mind had shut down, and her body got still. She repeatedly tried hard to collect herself but constantly failed; there was no one by her side. In the end, she closed her eyes, thought about Rahul, and prayed to God for courage in talking to her family.

She got a chance to talk to her mummy, and without wasting any time, she said, "Mummy, I am sorry, but I can't accept this alliance; I couldn't think of getting married to anyone else other than Rahul; I know you all are not okay with it, and I promise not to go against your wish and so will not marry him but getting into another relationship is also not possible, I am sorry I will not be able to take any step ahead."

Even before Mallvika could complete, everyone had heard it, and the room was filled with loud noises; there were showering of taunts and scoldings from every corner; Mallvika got blank, and couldn't hear or see what was happening around until it all got silent, It was like a heavy storm passed by.

All went out of the room, leaving her behind; it was like everyone had disowned her forever.

There was silence for hours, which was broken by Praveen, "Just leave her here and let's all go; she is capable of doing things on her own, she will find out a way for herself, she doesn't need us and so do we" There had been a lot of discussion and arguments going on, Suryakant too decided to go back to Madras.

   Destiny and Karma: Hand in Hand

CHAPTER 7

Is it the End of the Innocent Love Story

The Vora family was very angry with Mallvika, and everyone taunted her for being so rude, uncaring, and disrespectful. None of them wanted to talk to her, and it was as if they had literally abandoned her. Suryakant was feeling so very insulted and decided to leave for Madras as he was not interested in creating any more scenes in their relative's house. It was decided to turn up to Madras, leaving Mallvika behind. Jasumati and Suryakant, being parents, couldn't take this and decided Mallvika's return with them .

Mallvika felt extremely sorry about her behaviour, and even though she had no such intention, she was left with no choice. She never in her dreams had thought things would go this way.

The Vora's were back to Madras. There was no conversation between them for a day, then Suryakant ultimately decided to talk to Mallvika, "We have lost all our prestige and reputation because of you; we will not be able to face society anymore now what are your plans; why are you here, why don't you leave my house?"

Mallvika, with guilt and regret in her voice, said, "Pappa, I had never wished to disrespect you and believe me, I have tried my best not to indulge myself in any such acts that will hurt you."

Mallvika had decided to tell the truth and not misguide her parents anymore despite the fact that it was not the right time, as the duos had decided to wait till Ripun's wedding.

Before Mallvika could disclose her thoughts, Suryakant said," I want to give you a last chance; either do as we say, or if you choose to be with Rahul, you can leave this house, which will result at the end of my life. I can't face disgrace and dishonour anymore. You know me well, so don't consider this to be a hollow threat.

Malvika was shocked and terrified. She was very scared and questioned herself, "Does Pappa mean what he just said? If he hurts himself, then what? If something really goes wrong, then?"

She was not able to make any decisions. She had neither got a chance to inform Rahul nor to decide on what to do. It was like a dead-end, but she took the courage to tell the truth and politely responded, "Pappa, I promise I will never hurt you, and I will never choose to get married to Rahul against your wish. I will not be the reason to bring down

Destiny and Karma: Hand in Hand

your name and reputation, but at the same time, I can't think of getting married to anyone else, so I request you to please stop looking for a match for me, and I assure that I will never ever go against you and marry Rahul. Instead, I will stay with you forever.

Suryakant instantly reacted with extreme anger, "You have gone totally blind and crazy, but I can't endure this; you can do whatever you like, and now I very well know what I should be doing; I can't stand to face notoriety and infamy caused by you." With this, he ran to the washroom to get phenol; everything was happening at the speed of light, and the family members ran behind him. Mallvika was stunned and froze, trying to collect what exactly had happened; by the time she realised and could react, her family had gotten caught in Suryakant, and all were trying to control him.

Mallvika was very disturbed by the act that had just happened and blamed herself for it. She lost her mind, and the ambiance around pushed her to do the act that she would never do. She, out of depression and frustration, spoke to herself, "No one other than me should be punished for the act I have done; I am responsible for all this mess, and if this has to be cleaned up only with someone's death than it has to be mine" with this going in her head she landed doing something which she didn't believe in. She ran to the washroom and consumed phenol within a fraction of a moment.

Everyone was with Suryakant; none of them were aware of what Mallvika had done.

Mallvika was feeling guilty about spoiling every life close to her; she had never thought or believed in taking such steps as she always believed in fighting hard. Mallvika thought her parents would be free from the pain that she had given them for the past three years, but at the same time, she was in so much pain for losing all the dreams that the duos had seen together and felt very guilty about leaving Rahul halfway, she so very wished, she could see or say goodbye to Rahul, her heart was wishing for a last glance of her beloved. With this dream in her eyes, she started feeling unconscious.

By now, Suryakant was controlled and calmed by the family members. Jasumati, who was equally worried for Mallvika, searched for her but couldn't see her around; she then got up to look for her, even though she didn't feel like leaving Suryakant. She went near the washroom; she lost her breath as she saw Mallvika unconscious on the floor. She screamed and jumped to Mallvika; all the family members rushed there; it did not take any moment to understand what had happened.

 Destiny and Karma: Hand in Hand

CHAPTER 8

Ego or Concern

Jasumati was terrified seeing Mallvika on the floor; she cried out loud for help. A few family members tried to regain consciousness while others were trying to puke the chemical out; they were rushed to the hospital for a total cleanup.

An hour later, things were under control; Mallvika was still in the unconscious stage, repeatedly blabbering Rahul's name; Jasumati was right next to her, noticing her unconscious acts.

Jasumati, being a mother, couldn't take this anymore and decided to support Mallvika's genuine love for Rahul as she had seen no fault in the relationship. Jasumati had kept quiet and supported the family for their unreasonable opposition, but not anymore. Jasumati had planned to convince Suryakant. She knew it would take time, but she would succeed.

Rahul was unaware of the total situation. In fact, he had no idea of the engagement episode, was not aware of Mallvika's return to Madras, and did not have any knowledge of Mallvika's hospitalisation. They last got connected when Mallvika had to leave Ahmedabad. After that, the twosome had no communication bridge. Rahul was eagerly waiting to get over with Ripun's wedding, as he could then talk to both families about their marriage. He knew his proposal would bring a lot of complications, and that's why he wanted to get over with the wedding, as he did not wish to be the reason for spoiling Ripun's special day.

Everything seemed to be deadlocked. For a few days, there was total stillness. All were busy in their own ways to solve the problem; Jasumati was working on convincing Suryakant by repeatedly pointing out the good qualities of Rahul and the Tolia family. She pointed out, "The only reason I could understand is that Tolias are not as financially strong with regards to our expectations, but they are definitely well to do, and with all three capable sons, their growth is definite. I don't understand what's the real reason for opposing; it looks like more of an ego than the concern,"

Jasumati took a pause and continued, "Besides this, there is nothing that could be pointed out against them. We shared the same caste and community, we know the family well, and we had such good relations; we have known Rahul since his teens;

he is such a decent boy, and for the past two years, we have also been aware of his career growth, then what is it for us to oppose." Jasumati, trying to understand the reaction, continued," I understand you want the best for our daughter, but do you realise for Mallvika, Rahul is best." Most prominently, she kept saying," We were lucky this time that nothing happened to Mallvika, but we may not be lucky every time."

Whereas Suryakant was thinking of various ways to convince Mallvika as he couldn't go against Praveen, even though Jasumati's efforts made him realise Mallvika's deep love for Rahul, especially after her suicide attempt.

On the other end, Mallvika was desperately waiting for a chance to connect with Rahul and tell him about the hell of an experience she had faced the past few days.

During this standstill storm, Ripun's wedding was accomplished without any hindrance.

Mallvika also grabbed a chance to brief Rahul what had happened, and they had decided to talk to the families. Meanwhile, Jasumati's attempt was full-fledged, but yet there was no fruitful result.

Before Rahul could talk to the Vora family, uncle Praveen had played his cards. Once again, he came up with an alliance in Bombay. But this time, Mallvika decided to fight back and not leave Madras. She strongly opposed and clearly put up her decision not to see any alliance. Praveen was not ready to give up even though he realised the acceptance of Rahul in Suryakant's eyes. He, in fact, called the Tolias and threatened the family with imprisonment of Rahul and the family against kidnapping their daughter.

Vinesh and Ranjula got very scared and wanted to safeguard their son,

Other family members couldn't take this; they got furious and, full of hatred in their hearts, decided to convince Rahul to back-off, in spite of their awareness that Rahul would never agree to it.

Now, it was Tolia's turn to play emotionally and stop Rahul.

Chetan spoke to Rahul," Rahul, you very well know we never had any objection to your relationship with Mallvika, but not anymore, definitely not at the cost of your life."

Rahul replied with disappointment in his tone, "Yes, Bhaiyla, I can understand the Vora family had objections from day one and have not missed any chance of showing their hatred, but as you said, our family never had any objection, then why was there no act of support? He continued," Anyway, I have no hopes from anyone, and regardless of whatever happens, I am not going to quit; I will never leave Mallvika; even if they kill me, it's fine."

Chetan knew Rahul's weakness very well, and he exactly hammered on it.

Chetan said angrily," You are being selfish and thinking only about you and your relationship, but it's not about you; they have threatened us that they will put all of us behind bars. Do you understand that the entire family, including Pappa, has

                    Destiny and Karma: Hand in Hand

to go through this because of you and your act? It's enough now, right now you have to come with me and tell Mallvika that you are cutting off all the threads and will never ever see her again,"

Rahul kept the fighting spirit for a long time, but the family pressure and the threat to his family forced him to think, "Is Bhaiylo right? Am I being selfish? Am I thinking only about Mallvika? God forbid if something really goes wrong with the family, then what? And if I back-off, what about Mallvika, who stood against every allegation made, who believes and trusts me the most, who is fighting so hard for me, going through emotional and mental torture, humiliation, and separation? And how could I forget? She had just tried to give her life but had not given up on me. How can I leave her?" The fight was on for the day; none of them slept that night.

Rahul's mind was conquered by the continuous pressure; added to it was the breakdown of his father, which had forced him to finally agree to what Chetan wanted him to do.

CHAPTER 9

Coward or Altruistic

The next morning, Chetan called Jasumati and spoke to her about their coming; he requested Jasumati to come down with Mallvika at the entrance gate. Mallvika, unaware of what was going to happen, guessed the meeting to be the result of Rahul's convincing his family and felt so happy as she thought the meeting would be in favour of their togetherness. Full of excitement and hope at its peak, she left with Jasumati; her heart was beating faster and faster as she was nearing the gate; she could see Rahul from afar, and she locked her eyes on him; nothing else was visible to her.

Mallvika noticed Rahul was neither looking happy nor looking at her; his eyes were fixed on the ground, and it was very easy for Mallvika to understand that Rahul was feeling extremely guilty, but she couldn't identify why he looked culpable.

Chetan started the conversation. He spoke to Jasumati masi (Aunty) Rahul wanted to talk to Mallvika, and that's the reason I had called you people here; I know you don't favour this, yet you are here with Mallvika, but I believe me this meeting was very necessary. He then gazed at

Rahul and gave a hint to convey the message that they had come for. Rahul had no guts to look at Mallvika as he knew his eyes would speak the truth. He was also not ready to say anything, as his words would shatter her into pieces. Chetan tried all his strategies, but Rahul chose to stay quiet; his eyes were still stuck on the ground, and Mallvika's eyes was on him.

Chetan finally thought of transmitting the message himself, "Mallvika, Rahul is here to tell you that he is not interested anymore in this relationship and wants to stay away from you, and also wish the same from you."

Mallvika was not at all shocked as she strongly believed Rahul could never think of getting separated from her, but her eyes, with questions of what exactly happened, were yet at a standstill on Rahul.

Chetan continues," Rahul has now understood it was a big mistake, and he does not want to carry it forward. He feels it was an act of immaturity and more of infatuation, and he wants to rectify his mistake."

Mallvika, who was listening to Chetan's meaningless words, had no doubts in her eyes, which were still on Rahul. Rahul had no courage to look at Mallvika as he knew she would read the truth in his eyes, and his motive would fail.

Chetan was now provoked by the silent action of the duos, none of them were showing any response, his voice and actions now raised with anger and he pulled Rahul from his hands and commanded him to speak, he looked into

Rahul's eyes and secretly passed the message of threat to their family.

Rahul had no choice and finally spoke with total remorse in his voice, "Whatever bhaiyla said is true; I am sorry," was the only sentence from his mouth that came out.

Mallvika was not ready to buy his words; she had yet not lost her faith in Rahul, but Jasumati had reacted with extreme hatred and screamed at Mallvika, saying, "This is the person right in front of you for whom you were insanely mad at and also had made all of us crazy. In fact, I feel so stupid that I was trying so hard for this boy to be accepted." Do you have anything more to listen to, or will you still behave foolishly."

Mallvika's trust was still resolute, and her eyes were still on Rahul. Chetan could see Mallvika had not believed a word that was told, and this was making him more furious. He then screamed at Mallvika," We have said what we wanted to. It's not our problem if you believe it or not, but from now onwards, I don't want you to bother Rahul." on this, Mallvika spoke to Rahul, ignoring Chetan as she wanted to show it's between two of us and no one should come in between, "Rahul if you want me to believe in the nonsense that was just uttered, then talk to me with eye contact, "Chetan very well knew, Rahul will never do that and so he thought smart and wanted to leave. But Rahul, being altruistic, had something else in his mind; he spoke to Mallvika from deep inside with extreme pain in his voice yet politeness in his tone.

"MALLVIKA, USUALLY PEOPLE SAY LOVE IS BLIND, AND WE ALSO COULD NOT SEE ANYTHING ELSE IN OUR LOVE; WE ONLY LOOKED AT EACH OTHER AND DID NOT REALISE IF SOMEONE WAS SAD OR SOMEONE WAS HURT OR SOMEONE WAS LOSING HIS LIFE... I HAD PROMISED YOU ON THE DAY ONE THAT I COULDN'T HURT OTHERS FOR OUR UNION; INSTEAD, I WOULD CHOOSE TO HURT MYSELF, AND I WILL KEEP UP WITH THE PROMISE MADE." Rahul conveyed his feelings, and at that moment, Mallvika couldn't understand as she was badly hurt; she was terribly terrified by what Rahul had said. Her mind was angry, but her heart was in denial mode; she couldn't control her pain and had confounded Rahul to the core.

Rahul, in his mind, "Usually, most of the time, men say out of horniness, bravado, and stupidity, but I had hurt her intentionally."

Rahul felt happy, he wanted Mallvika to hate him as that will be the easiest way for her to get over him.

Before anything else could take place, Chetan pulled Rahul and said, "We are done with what we had to say; let's go now."

Rahul knew this was his last meeting, as he had his own plan of action. He wanted to have his last glimpse at Mallvika, he looked up to her with passion and Mallvika could read a lot in his eyes but before she could understand Chetan grabbed Rahul and left.

Chetan, on their way back, tried emotionally manipulating Rahul, but Rahul couldn't hear a word; his mind was occupied with Mallvika's thoughts and was waiting to reach home for his plan to be executed.

The previous day had thrown a lot of complications and problems that couldn't be resolved. Rahul had thought hard for a solution all night, but nothing was coming up against the safety of both families. Rahul's decision to talk to Suryakant masa was also not worth it; it was too late now as the situation was out of control, and it has now reached legal action. Rahul, as always believed not to hurt others, had decided to harm himself, and with this decision, he had agreed to meet Mallvika. His intention was to hurt Mallvika with his words and actions, which would result in hatred; it would be easy for Mallvika to move on.

Rahul went straight to his room, locked himself, and instructed his family not to distribute as he wanted to spend some time alone. He had his plan ready to perform. He had consumed the harmful chemicals, which would quickly take his breath off.

The Tolias were worried as they knew how emotional Rahul was and would tend to harm himself; they knocked on the door and asked Rahul to open it. Rahul repeated himself," I don't want to talk to anyone; please leave me alone. Tolias waited and thought he would come out soon. Sometime later, they could sense something was wrong; they had not wasted any moment further and started pushing the door harder and harder. Their tries failed, and the family panicked as there was no sign of any response from Rahul. It was time for quick action, and every member of the Tolia family was involved in crashing the door; they soon succeeded. Rahul had accomplished his plans and was lying on the bed. They ran to check his pulse, and they were happy; they could feel a weak pulse; the family thanked God for not being late and quickly rushed to the hospital. Destiny had some other plans and Rahul was now safe.

WHEN A MAN TRULY LOVES A WOMAN, SHE BECOMES HIS WEAKNESS. WHEN A WOMAN LOVES A MAN, HE BECOMES HER STRENGTH. THIS IS CALLED EXCHANGE OF POWER.

CHAPTER 10

Love Never Gives Up

A true relationship is two imperfect people refusing to give up on each other.

Mallvika was standing there and wishing for Rahul to turn back, she stood until Rahul vanished from his sight. Mallvika still did not believe in any of the words spoken, she so very wished it to be a bad dream, which will break soon.

Jasumati dragged Mallvika back home as Mallvika was not in her senses.

She was eternally fighting with her mind, punching her hard, and saying Rahul had backed off while her heart was pampering by convincing her that "Rahul will never ever leave her; there was definitely something that compelled Rahul to react this way. If I don't understand Rahul, then who could?" The fight was long and went on for almost five hours. Finally, the heart had victory over the mind. She spoke to herself," Rahul had fulfilled his promise of not hurting others; he always believed in altruistic behaviour. Now it's my turn to fulfil the promise I made, "I will never give up on Rahul and will never give up on our union." With this thought, Mallvika decided to leave the house with no sense of surety.

She quietly left the house but Jasumati and her aunt who were sitting on their balcony saw her going, they screamed and called her back but Mallvika had not responded, Jasumati ran behind to stop her but Mallvika caught an auto and was soon out of Jasumati's sight.

Mallvika had left the house with no plans. She had no idea of what would happen, she questioned herself," I have left my house for the person who broke all relations with me, I even have no surety whether Rahul will be with me or not? On what basis am I taking such a severe step? What if Rahul really denies our relationship? What will I do?" Despite all the doubts, her inner conscience encouraged her to proceed.

YOU CAN'T JUST GIVE UP ON SOMEONE JUST BECAUSE THE SITUATIONS ARE NOT IDEAL. GREAT RELATIONSHIP ARE NOT GREAT BECAUSE THEY HAVE NO PROBLEMS. THEY ARE GREAT BECAUSE BOTH PEOPLE CARE ENOUGH ABOUT THE OTHER PERSON TO FIND A WAY TO MAKE IT WORK.

Mallvika hadn't decided where she was heading; she just sat in an auto and moved on. She wanted to go straight to Rahul, but very well knew going to Rahul's house would be a disaster. Mallvika then recalled that Rahul had once shown her Ranish's house and had told her to go there in case of any emergency. She decided to go there; on the way, she felt very awkward as she knew Ranish only through Rahul's conversation. She had met him only once, but she did not think much as she had no other option.

The two started their journey forty months ago and continuously travelled on a very difficult path; they had crossed many hurdles successfully. They hoped that now it was time for the final destination, but they were totally unaware of the toughest hurdle that was coming up.

Mallvika was clueless about Rahul's condition.

Mallvika reached Ranish's residence but had not seen or met Ranish's wife Rupali before, it was a very uncomfortable situation. She introduced herself and requested to call Ranish for further explanation. Rupali called Ranish, he immediately spoke to Mallvika and consoled her, he also informed that he will reach there soon and then will work on what has to be done. Ranish also instructed Rupali to make Mallvika feel comfortable.

Rupali and other family members created a very soothing and warm atmosphere for Mallvika to feel better.

Ranish arrived in no time; he then called Rahul to inform him about Mallvika and decide on how to proceed. The call was answered by Chetan, and he informed Ranish about Rahul being hospitalised. Ranish was stunned and couldn't say anything; he then just told Chetan," I'm coming."

He told Mallvika to come with him; on the way, Ranish briefed her about their visit to the hospital and what had happened and also consoled her that Rahul was safe now. All the way through, Mallvika was thinking about Rahul and his altruistic nature. She could understand Rahul's situation as she had been through the same circumstance a few days back.

As Mallvika and Ranish entered the hospital, Chetan and Reena stopped them. Mallvika requested," Reena, bhabhi please allow me to see him once; I will not leave without meeting him. "She made Mallvika sit beside her and said," Mallvika, I can very well understand what you are going through; believe me, Rahul is fine, but if you meet him now, he may get emotional and could again do something wrong. Let him recover, wait for a day or two, and it's my promise to you that I will get you both together."

Mallvika, who was not willing to leave, couldn't deny Reena's request and left with Ranish. Mallvika now had to wait for Rahul to be back home, and until then, nothing could be done, so she requested Ranish to book a hotel for her stay. Ranish instantly said no," Mallvika, I have to keep you safe. You are my responsibility until I bring Rahul and you together. Rahul had trusted me, and that's why he told you to come to me in such a situation. I can never break his trust; you are going to stay with us." She couldn't say anything and agreed to stay at his place.

It looked like the storm had settled, and the bright days were ahead, but Mallvika's destiny was tough, and her exams were getting tougher at every level. "It was the peace before the heavy storm."

The Vora family was aggressively looking for Mallvika, they had started looking for her at every possible place, they had called and checked each and every friend of Rahul that Kalpesh knew. Kalpesh could get information from a few others, where it was possible for Mallvika to go. Finally, they came to know about Mallvika's stay at Ranish house.

Ranish had an idea that such a thing might happen, so he had already gathered his Honda gang. The Vora's came in a group and fought aggressively. Things went beyond the limit, and so Ranish had to file a police complaint against Vora for forcefully getting into their residence. The Vora's were very influential and had filed a complaint of kidnapping their daughter.

Things became dirty. Everyone in the Honda gang, including Mallvika, was scared, but Ranish had not given up. He then first spoke to Mallvika," Mallvika, things are getting legal, and what's your call now? Do you want to continue with the fight or want to surrender? Everything depends on you; if you are ready to fight to any extent, I promise we all will be standing and supporting you, and your victory is definite. But yes, you can't afford to lose your confidence." Mallvika thought for a while and said," I will stay strong and will work hard towards my destiny, but I 'm scared of all of you as I know my family; they will use all their influence to break us down, and I can't harm any of you for my benefits. Above all, Rahul is in hospital, and he has no idea what's happening." Ranish replied, "It's good that Rahul is in hospital; the police can't file anything against him." He further explained the scenario, "They can only file a complaint saying we have kidnapped you, but if you give you witness saying you are major and have rights to take a decision and it's your decision to leave the house." With this statement of yours, they can't touch any of us.

Mallvika never ever thought of standing against the family. She was now very much disturbed as her family was so much into satisfying their ego that they couldn't see anything; they were not concerned about any emotions; their only consideration was that things should happen as they wanted. I would have definitely done whatever they said, but their opposition is so baseless that they couldn't prove a single fault in Rahul.

And now, this police case, an extreme action that is usually taken against an enemy, has forced me to rebel.

Mallvika, with the Honda gang, had to be present at the police station as the complaint was filed. The scenes at the station were very nasty, filthy, and crummy. The police had their list of questions, which were answered well, as Ranish had already prepared all of them. The police couldn't find any fault, they couldn't do anything legal, and so neither could they force Malvika to return home nor could they create any scene at Ranish's residence.

Mallvika was back with Ranish at his residence. They could now breathe with ease as there was no more legal risk.

CHAPTER 11

Few Favouring Stars By Their Side

On the other end, Rahul was not aware of anything as he had just been discharged. The first thing he did as soon as he entered the house was to call Naresh to get to know about Mallvika; how was she? Was everything fine with her or not? Is she safe and stable? He was worried about the complications that could have happened due to his back-off act. But Rahul couldn't connect to him.

Reena was watching this and she decided to tell Rahul about what all had happened in the past two days. She started right from Mallvika's strong belief in him and his love; she eloped from the house, went to Ranish's house, came to the hospital, and made her promise to Mallvika of their togetherness. She did not miss out on anything.

Reena was not aware of anything about the chaos at Ranish residence, the police complaint, the police station scene, so Rahul couldn't get any of that information.

Rahul just moved ahead to go to Ranish house to see Mallvika but Reena stopped him and she told," I remember my promise given to Mallvika of getting you both together. I will talk to masa and ask for Mallvika alliance for you, till then I don't want you to get into any other trouble and further spoil the situation." Rahul believed and agreed to it.

Jasumati had gone wild with the police station actions, she spoke to Suryakant," what is happening is not right, we are fighting a nasty battle against our own daughter, it's disgusting, and the battle is just to win over our ego and no concern is seen."

Suryakant, who was shaken up by the police station act, was trying to understand what Jasumati had told him.

Jasumati then looked at Suryakant, who was quietly listening with an expression of acceptance. She further said," Above all, for the past three years, we have tried all the tactics to break them apart but failed at every point, and now this police case, does it suit us? We have gone down so much just to satisfy our ego. By now, we should realise that they are inseparable. It's enough now; I'm not going to take this anymore. I can't afford to lose my daughter. I have decided to get Mallvika married to Rahul, and I wish you to support me as I always stand by you; if not, you may lose me too."

Jasumati had very clearly conveyed her decision, and Suryakant's thoughts also diverged and agreed to stand by Jasumati's decision.

Meanwhile Suryakant had asked one of his friends Amu bhai to call Mallvika and convince her to come back home, he also promised that he will get them married. Mallvika had a lot of respect for Uncle Amu; she believed his words and headed toward her house.

The Vora family was finally convinced other than uncle Praveen; he had not given up yet. The Vora family was planning how to proceed while uncle Praveen was thinking in a totally opposite direction. He now spoke to Kalpesh," Kalpesh, If the wedding is organised, you have to put down all your friends, who will not miss any chance to insult you. Will you be able to take any such disgrace?" Uncle Praveen had always managed to influence Kalpesh and had not missed out on it even now. Kalpesh was influenced by Praveen's words, and now we had a new hurdle to cross.

Reena decided she was there to meet Mallvika's parents. She preferred to have no middlemen, as she believed they were the ones who always created more conflicts, and so she chose to directly speak to them," Masa, masi (uncle and aunty), I have come here to ask for Mallvika's alliance for Rahul, and if you are not okay with this, please let me know what the problem is. I will do my best to overcome the problem, as I can't see Rahul and Mallvika suffering anymore. They had gone through a lot. We are lucky that in spite of their suicide attempts, we have them with us, but we may not be lucky every time."

Suryakant who was already convinced, was happy to see someone from Rahul's side coming up with an alliance, as it gives surety and a sense of security for Mallvika. He then showed his approval with tears in his eyes and a smile on his face.

The twosome had always managed to sail safe from the regular accruing storms in their love life. The time had come for the duos to get their answer to the Love, dedication, confidence, respect, hard work, belief, patience, honesty, and the various ways of prayer they had shown over the past 40 months.

Suryakant who was convinced was now thinking if the wedding was to be organised then they may lose their son Kalpesh, so he thought long and came to conclusions of register marriage, where there will be no interaction and so there will be no chance of any conflict.

So finally, the wedding was fixed with a unique style of that era, yes in '90s in India there were only two types of marriages happening, either arranged marriages with parents blessings and full-fledged celebration or love marriages where the couple elope and get married in court without parents' permission where the friends signed the witness box, but our story was unique and so was the wedding.

It was decided that despite their parents' blessings, they would not witness the wedding. The couple, with other family members, will go to the court; the couple will sign before the registrar, where close family members will sign as the witnesses, a totally unique wedding.

Rahul and Mallvika were not bothered by the way it was happening as they were extremely happy about their togetherness with the blessings of their elders, for which they had gone through a hell of experiences.

It was exactly the way they had promised,

"RAHUL HAD PROMISED NOT TO HURT ANYONE FOR THEIR UNION; INSTEAD, HE WILL HARM HIMSELF, AND MALLVIKA HAD PROMISED NOT TO STEP BACK, HOWEVER HARD THE FIGHT BE."

It's always seen that the couples have opposite personalities, and it was so very true in this case ….

RAHUL BELIEVED IN DESTINY," WHAT IS MINE WILL DEFINITELY COME TO ME "

MALLVIKA BELIEVED IN KARMA,

"WITHOUT WORKING HARD, WE CAN'T ACHIEVE, EVEN THOUGH IT IS IN OUR DESTINY."

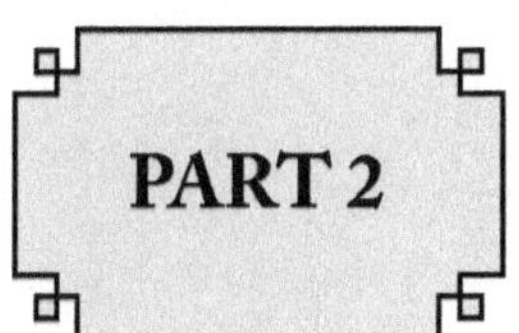

Was it up or was it down,

The circle of fate was always on its
round...

Was it loss or was it profit

The twosome always won the

trophy....

Was it past or was it future,

The duos were always meant to be
together.....

CHAPTER 12

The Harder the Struggle, the More Glorious the Triumph

So true is the saying, "The fruit of patience is sweet," and here in this love story, it's not only patience. There were lots and lots that had gone in to finally taste the fruit of togetherness to be sweet.

Rahul and Mallvika had not yet come out of the trauma that they had just overcome. The past encounters had killed the feeling of excitement of their wedding. Instead they were more scared, as they had experienced disasters whenever they had experienced a moment of happiness. Regardless of all the ambivalent (mixed feelings) the most awaited day of their life had come.

Jasumati had arranged a part of it that was given to a bride at her wedding, right from jewellery to outfits, in spite of the short available span of just 24 hrs. Every girl has a dream of her wedding, a grand celebration with all rituals and blessings, the most important day of her life. But Mallvika had given up on all the dreams; she only wanted to be with Rahul forever. Mallvika was not interested in what and how the wedding was organised, as her mind was totally engrossed in its accomplishment.

The Tolia family were also getting ready to welcome Mallvika even though it had no sign of excitement. On the contrary, Rahul also was only interested in their conjoin, and nothing else mattered to him. He was accompanied to the registrar's office by his brothers, sisters-in-law, cousins, and friends. The only group that looked excited were his friends.

Mallvika was there with her cousins and a few elders from the family. She was given a warm farewell from her residence by her parents and a few other family members.

Rahul and Mallvika looked so worried and nervous. They hardly looked at each other; the only thing going in their minds were the prayers "PRAYERS OF THEIR ONENESS."

The signing procedure was done, and the couple exchanged the garlands, and yes, the duos were tied together forever. The struggle for their unity was over, and the stamp of oneness was sealed on their relationship. Rahul's belief in DESTINY was proved right, and Mallvika's KARMA paid off.

Rahul and Mallvika were still in an unacceptable zone, but deep inside, they were so happy, in spite of there being no smile on their faces, as the recent trauma had left a very hard impact on both. The friends could sense the pressure that the couple was going through, they soon created an atmosphere of happiness, achievement and excitement which finally lightened the ambiance.

The newly wedded couple was welcomed by the Tolia family through a few welcoming rituals performed by Reena and Riddhi. The stress was still in the atmosphere, but the continuous approach of Naresh, Ranish, Keyur, and a few others had succeeded in de-stressing the same.

The couple was meeting after the "break-up" acts took place four days ago. The span was short, but numerous series of awful events took place. In a normal scenario, it was time for them to talk about all those events, especially for Mallvika, who actually deserved an answer for Rahul's ditching and the suicide act.

But this story was not normal, and so its actions were abnormal, too....

The twosome kept in silence for long, and again the duos with totally different personalities thought and acted in their own ways.

Rahul's guilt was not allowing him to look up to Mallvika, while Mallvika, who had forgotten about all the previous nasty acts, was feeling shy to look up to Rahul.....Rahul had no explanation for the actions he performed whereas Mallvika had no questions regarding those actions.....Rahul couldn't cut him off from the past, on the contrary Mallvika was looking forward in life.

Opposite personalities often balance each other. As long as there is mutual respect and love, and neither one tries to impose their way on the other, it shouldn't be a problem.

True love involves knowing your partner inside out—their feelings, joys, and reactions. It goes beyond apologies and centres on mutual understanding and acceptance. This profound knowledge of each other creates a strong bond, allowing you to navigate challenges with empathy and support.

The couplets were extremely different in minds yet deeply similar in hearts. Besides this dissociative personality, their connection grew stronger as they succeeded in every obstacle that came their way.

It means literally that hard work pays off and one evolves in life after overcoming struggles of life. Just like gold turns into beautiful ornaments after burning in fire.

Destiny and Karma: Hand in Hand

KHUSH THO PEHLE BHI THE HUM,
JAB NAHI MILE THE TUM,
AUR JINDAGI HO GAYI HASEEN HAMARI,
JAB SE MILE HO TUM.
SHEKADO JATAN KIYE HUMNE,
JAB JAANA NAHI HO TAKDIR MAI TUM,
AUR KOSHISH NAHI CHODI HUMNE,
JAB TAK HUWE NA HAMARE TUM.
MUKADAR MAI SHAYAD NA THE TUM,
JAB DUR HO GAYE HUM TUM,
AUR PHICHE PAD GAYE HUM RAB KE,
JAB TAK RAB SE MILE NA TUM.
PUJA, PATH, VRAT AUR TYAG,
JAB KIYA SAB TAKI MILO TUM,
AUR RAB SE JESIE JANG KI HAMNE,
JAB TAK HASHIL HUYE NA TUM.
NASEEB SE YA KARAM SE,
JAB MIL GAYE TUM,
AUR RAB SE KIYA SHUKARIYA HAMNE,
JAB HO GAYE TUMHARE HUM AUR HAMARE TUM.

Soon the couple with unspoken words got connected leaving behind all the questions, complaints, heartburn, resentment, guilt, just by exchanging a promise of eternal bliss of togetherness. With this promise they had entered into the most awaited phase of their life.

Rahul wanted to compensate for the bitter past with a promise," Mallu I want to start our married life with a promise of giving you all the happiness and fill your life with endless love." Mallvika replies, "Rahul I too promise to stand by your side for the rest of my life."

Rahul and Mallvika quickly recovered from the trauma, and the twosome was back sailing together in the ocean of love after a long struggle of forty months. Once again, the past experience of their teenage love was back as though they had just fallen in love. They had also continued with the sweet daily routine custom they had started and promised at the time of their commitment,

"Farewell with a smile saying, have a good day ahead and a cordial welcome with a smile asking how the day was", the only changes were, it was no more secretive and there was no requirement of hints and clues like smashing the door or honking the bike.

Everything between the two was more than awesome, although some level of struggle between the families was on. The Vora's had not yet accepted the couple wholeheartedly, and so the Tolias were also not ready to initiate any relationship from their side and also restricted Mallvika to some extent, as they believed "if Mallvika will continue any kind of connection then the Vora's will never welcome Rahul." It was like "turning the table." The hidden fight between the families was endured.

    Destiny and Karma: Hand in Hand

A week later, the Tolia family purchased an engagement ring for Mallvika, and the rings between the two were exchanged a week after their wedding; everything was so unique in Mallvika and Rahul's lives.

Even though things were not great with family, life with friends was awesome. Rahul and Mallvika organised a day picnic with all their friends as a celebration and vote of thanks for being on their side during the toughest time of their lives. The picnic was full of fun, and each and everyone was so very happy for the conjoin of Rahul and Mallvika, but there were a few who were not only immensely happy but had promised to be their side for a lifetime, and the bunch included Ranish, Rupali, Keyur, Naresh, Veeraj and Yusuf.

Meanwhile Jasumati was going through health issues and her blood pressure had been showing unstable reading, Mallvika when acquired the news, wanted to visit but there was a discussion over the topic and it was not flavouring Mallvika, while Rahul felt it was not right, and had convinced the family for their visit as it was about the health issues. Rahul and Mallvika had visited Jasumati for a while, which had given a big relief to her.

From the Vora's side, Jasumati was trying hard to convince Suryakant to accept candidly, saying, "If we delay, then it will become difficult to patch, and with increasing time, the gap will get deeper, "but there were no such acts from Tolias.

Things escalated during Raksha Bandhan. Dhiraj was in Madras, and the argument went on in both families. Tolias wanted "a proper invitation for the couple only than Mallvika should go to tie Rakhi to Dhiraj," and Vora's had their perspective," Dhiraj is here, and Mallvika is not restricted to come, it should be her choice to come and tie Rakhi" Nothing was resolved, and the time went on, it was time for Dhiraj to catch his train. Rahul had finally decided to go to the railway station to tie Rakhi away from all kinds of disputes.

The couple's fight for their rights was not yet over, and it was like their struggle would have no end.

Rahul and Mallvika were getting things in parts, but they had no complaints as no materialistic things mattered to them; in fact, they took it as a non-stop celebration of their life. It was time for the mangalsutra ceremony; the Tolia family had purchased daily wear ornaments and a mangalsutra. As per the rituals, the mangalsutra was tied, and the two who were traumatised at the time of the wedding appreciated these little moments.

During the wedding, ornaments and outfits are given to the bride from the groom's side. Tolias, as per the rituals, had given these things to both daughters-in-law at their wedding, and now it was Mallvika's turn. The only difference was Mallvika was getting it in parts, and it did not matter the duos, or maybe they had not even realised that as they were too young for all these.

The couple couldn't yet go for their honeymoon due to the stress between the families, but it was trivial and unimportant to them, and there was no sign of inadequacy, as every moment of being together was like they were totally engrossed in each other, nothing less than a honeymoon.

Despite the tension between the families, Rahul and Mallvika's love only grew stronger. They found joy in their daily routines, and their bond deepened with every passing day. They faced each challenge together, supporting each other through the ups and downs. Their friends remained a constant source of support and happiness, helping them navigate the rough patches.

As time went on, the couple continued to build their life together, cherishing every moment and creating new memories. They knew that their journey was far from over, but they were ready to face whatever came their way, hand in hand, with love and determination guiding them forward.

CHAPTER 13

The News is....Good or Bad

It was almost two months, and life was beautiful between the two. It was like they were falling more and more for each other as the days passed.

Mallvika looked very tense and sad; she was very restless and was waiting for Rahul to come back home.

Rahul was back home, but the cordial welcome smile looked tense; Rahul could understand something was wrong; the stress and anxiety on Mallvika's face were overseen through the smile. Rahul wanted to find out what was wrong, but Mallvika asked him to wait until after dinner.

During the family dinner, neither of them could eat much due to the anxiety. As soon as dinner was over, they excused themselves, claiming to be tired, and retreated to their room.

Rahul immediately hugged Mallvika and gently asked her what was wrong. Mallvika couldn't hold back her emotions any longer and started crying. Rahul let her release her anxiety through tears. After a while, he made Mallvika sit down and sat beside her, looking into her eyes. "What happened, Mallu? Tell me... everything will be fine. We have gone through so much, and we will get through this, too. Tell me, Mallu, what's the matter?"

Mallvika held Rahul's hand and spoke with deep disappointment in her voice, "Rahul, we have just started our life. I just want to be with you all the time. I want to make up for each day of our separation." She stopped, unable to control her sobs.

Rahul took over, "Yes, Mallu, we are together now, and we will not only make up for lost time, but nothing can separate us anymore. Tell me the matter, and we will find a solution together."

With pain in her voice, Mallvika said, "Rahul, I am pregnant." Rahul was shocked for a moment and then laughed, "Mallu, are you mad? Were you crying over this? You scared me so much!"

Mallvika reacted, "Are you not scared? We are too young. I am just twenty, and you are twenty-two. We have just started our life together, and we were anxiously waiting to spend time without any kind of hindrance."

Rahul interrupted," I understand we have waited long for being together and we are and will always be together, the baby will be a strong link and not hindrance between us and yes, I agree we are too young, and it's not right time and most of all it's a huge responsibility, I feel I have not yet fully taken your responsibility and an added one, it scares me too but as always you being my side everything will be fine."

He kissed her forehead and hugged her tightly. Rahul had managed to console Mallvika, but deep down, he, too, was a bit worried. The reality of their situation weighed heavily on both of them, but their love and support for each other gave them the strength to face whatever lay ahead.

The couple was not very happy; they had just come out of a difficult period and wanted to enjoy their togetherness. For a while, Rahul and Mallvika felt depressed, with various concerns running through their minds. They were too young to handle the title "PARENTS." However, Rahul, with his belief in DESTINY, reassured her, saying, "God has a plan behind every act. He will also give us the strength to carry it well. Don't worry."

The strained relationship between the families persisted until the good news of their expecting a new bundle of joy was announced. Both families were extremely happy, as it was going to be the first baby of the generation on both sides. The news of being grandparents had cleaned up all the negativity, and everything between the families had changed in an instant.

Rahul and Mallvika were extremely happy to see the news have reunited the two families, something that had seemed impossible before. The baby's entry into their life brought them immense luck. It was like an angel had turned her magical wand, filling their lives with an ecstatic and blissful environment.

Everything was going extremely well; the couplets were at their best, and Rahul's career was reaching new heights.......

Mallvika, Reena, and Riddhi were bonding well; they tried a lot of new things together right from recipes to gossiping.....the grandparents were eagerly waiting for their grandchild.... and most importantly, life with friends, the Honda gang, was like a "feather on a cap," especially the bonding grew stronger with Ranish and Rupali, as others were yet bachelor.

★ ★ ★

As the families reunited, it was time for the lovebirds to go for their honeymoon," oh God, honeymoon with baby in the womb," something very unusual, just like their love story.

The couple went on a delayed honeymoon but were highly compensated with non-stop trips, which included only the couple's trips and the trips with friends. It was like they were on a weekend trip almost every month.

It was time for Navratri, the couple had enjoyed the festival, despite being three months pregnant, Mallvika had not missed any chance of playing raas garba. They fondly recalled the previous year's Navratri, which had its own special charm.

The couple not only managed the pregnancy period well but also continued to work towards their dream of living life in a certain way. Their efforts towards their goals were in full swing, balancing their new responsibilities and aspirations with grace and enthusiasm. Rahul always wanted Mallvika by his side wherever he went. If he could, he would have taken her to the trading floor, too. Rahul and his Honda gang had a routine of having lunch together every Saturday at either Rahul's or Naresh's office. It was usually a boys-only lunch, but Rahul started inviting Mallvika, who appreciated his efforts to spend more time together. She quickly became a regular at these lunches, making sure she was always available to be with him.

Mallvika made a routine of completing her necessary morning chores before Rahul woke up and finishing any pending household work during his business hours. She avoided any work when Rahul was home, as she wanted to spend every possible moment by his side.

The festival season arrived, and it was their first Diwali together. Rahul was excited and gifted Mallvika a saree and a small gold pendant set. It was the first gift from Rahul. Mallvika was thrilled, not just because of the gifts but because she was celebrating Diwali with Rahul.

Mallvika's family meant so much to her, but her one and only priority since she was sixteen was RAHUL, whereas Rahul had a list of priorities in his life, MALLVIKA, HIS FRIENDS, HIS FAMILY, AND HIS DREAM CAREER "SHARE TRADING" and he couldn't do without any of it. Mallvika knew his priorities very well, and soon, Mallvika could also connect well to all his priorities. Mallvika had already known all his friends, and now she was bonded so well that she was no longer a friend's wife; furthermore, she was one among them. Mallvika was equally indulged with the family members, and as she had known them all well for a long time, it became easy for them to gel. Regarding business, she couldn't be with him physically, but Rahul updated all the activities and kept Mallvika mentally involved. MALLVIKA'S LIFE ONLY REVOLVED AROUND RAHUL.

During the pregnancy period, they witnessed the conflict of being part of Kalpesh's engagement; Kalpesh was getting engaged to Rishita. Uncle Praveen had decided not to invite Mallvika, Rahul, and the Tolia family, as he believed in punishing her for the step she had taken. Once again, Jasumati had to lead the fight against unfairness and discrimination, and this time, she had the full support of Suryakant and Dhiraj. Praveen had to put his foot down, and despite his unwillingness, he had to invite the Tolia family. Things went well. In fact, Kalpesh's engagement was combined with a mini reception for Rahul and Mallvika, as the relatives were meeting them for the first time after their wedding.

It was time for Kalpesh and Rishita's wedding. Mallvika was in her third trimester, the sixth month. As her health was good, she could take part in full-fledged; the wedding was a grand celebration. The Tolia family had gotten a part of Mallvika's pending wedding gift, jewellery, and outfit during Kalpesh's wedding, and the balance may be in the near future; it had bothered Rahul and Mallvika for a while as it was supposed to be given fully and not partially on the day of their wedding, but they had let it go.

It was the seventh month of the pregnancy, time for the "shrimant," "baby shower," a moment of happiness in the duo's life without any conflicts, not possible. Tolias had their internal issues and things became nasty. The only function for Rahul and Mallvika, meant to be organised by the Tolia family, was at stake.

While the twosome was not deeply affected, it left a small mark on their hearts. They felt the family had not celebrated their wedding properly and could have at least arranged a small reception. However, the couple soon got over it.

After a few days of discussion and arguments, the function was on. All family members of both families and a few close relatives were invited to give their blessings to the baby in the womb.

A life without challenge, hardship, and purpose seems pale and pointless. With challenge comes perseverance and gumption. With hardship comes resilience and resolve. With purpose comes strength and understanding.

Mallvika was blessed with good health throughout her pregnancy period. It was Sunday, and as routine, the couple was out with their gang for dinner and beach. An hour after their return, Mallvika had labour pain, and she was taken to the hospital. There was a frisson of excitement in the warm air.

Mallvika endured labour pains throughout the night and into the next day, but there was no sign of relief. The situation became a bit nasty and risky. She was facing complications with a closed cervix, leading to the decision to go for a caesarean. It seemed nothing came easy in Mallvika's life; she had to go through serious hardships to achieve anything. She had to endure the pain of both labour and a caesarean in one pregnancy.

After a long wait of two days and two nights, the baby finally made her entry into the beautiful world. The couple was blessed with a healthy, cute little princess, the first child of the generation. This new addition brought immense joy and a sense of fulfilment, making all their struggles worthwhile.

CHAPTER 14

A Little Bit of Heaven in Our Arms

Love between parent and child is the highest experience and the closest to divine love.

When the baby was born, all the pain that was endured vanished in an instant. Love for that tiny baby made us forget all the pain and the fear we had the past two days.

The moment we saw our baby, we felt a different level of joy and excitement. We were exhilarated by seeing the baby and felt grateful for being parents.

When the little angel finally was placed into our arms, our joy was running down our eyes and our face sparked with a huge smile, we kissed her forehead with unsaid blessings, we looked into her precious eyes and felt an overwhelming, unconditional love....we never felt so complete and empowered in our life.

We felt a sense of achievement.

IT WAS LIKE A LITTLE BIT OF HEAVEN WAS SENT DOWN TO US.

Mallvika was feeling so blissful and wanted to thank Rahul for completing her," Rahul, motherhood is a blessing, and you made it possible; you have given me the privilege of being a mother; it's the greatest gift you could ever give me. We've journeyed through life together, and becoming parents is a new chapter. I am grateful for the beautiful life we have created. Thank you, my love."

Rahul, too, was so glad and delighted and expressed his feelings, "Mallu, I want to thank you from the bottom of my heart for being my partner, my confidante, my best friend, and now mother of our child.

You've gone through all the pain and have given me the opportunity to be called a father of such a cute princess, giving our love a new meaning. Being a father, I will need no reason to love my baby, yet you will be my inspiration to love because no matter what happens, this baby will be half of you. She will be everything that you are right now and more. I will be falling in sacred love with a part of you all over again, and "saying this, Rahul cuddles over Mallu and the baby with the utmost affection.

Rahul and Mallvika were so thankful to each other for making the momentous decision to have a baby, even though they panicked and were not ready at the beginning. It was like deciding forever to have your heart go walking around outside your body.

Everyone was extremely happy. The excitement of both families was at its peak. Friends, as usual, had added to the happiness of being beside them.

Ranjula was so very happy, and she thanked by saying "Mallu you have fulfilled my dreams of a daughter in the family, I'm so very happy and thankful." Suryakant and Jasumati thanked God for the good health of their daughter Mallvika and the newly born angel.

It was time for the naming ceremony for the angel. Rahul and Mallvika wanted a unique, short, and sweet name as they were not in favour of having any nickname for their princess. They had finally decided on a name," Neer; yes, the cute little bundle of joy was named "Neer, who had the power to dissolve everything and bring it to one solution.

Life is a mixture of periods of joy and sorrow. Develop the courage to welcome both with equal zeal.

Mother and daughter were home with more episodes of happiness and a few sad while Mallvika was in hospital. There were a few arguments within the family for Mallvika's stay as she had gone through a c-section, and there were some norms for her health to be followed for a month, and it was not supported well. Although Rahul and Mallvika had "let go" and decided to adjust, as usually nothing much bothered them when they were beside each other. This time, it was about the health of Mallvika, so there was a bitter pinch in their heart.

In this first month's process, Mallvika missed her mother Jasumati a lot as she had to be in Ahmedabad to settle down Kalpesh and Rishita, who had just started their newly married life, and there was also good news : Rishita was expecting.

The first few days experience with a newborn can leave you feeling sore, sleepy, and a little weepy. It could also feel like an emotional wreck and struggle to settle into a routine, but soon, we learn and feel a newborn can be blissful, anxiety-ridden, and especially when our partner is all the time beside us.

The newly-becoming parents were experiencing, enjoying, learning, and adapting to every little thing that was required to look after their princess. They were too young to be parents, but they soon self-learned the skills of parenthood with episodes of success and failures. Rahul and Mallvika participated equally in this learning process. In the '90s, the child was mainly brought up by the mother with elders in the family, and fathers had a very small role to play, but this was Rahul and Mallvika's story, and they had to win this battle too on their own abilities, people were all around, but the struggle was only in their plate. They happily stood by each other's side even at this stage of their life. They took up the challenge and succeeded well. Rahul stood by Mallvika during the first month, which is the most crucial period; he was there right from taking the baby from the cradle to supporting her back while in a sitting position, lulling the baby to sleep, changing the nappies and staying awake through every sleepless night. The parenthood had brought them even closer; it was an added ring to the chain of their bonding.

IT WAS THE TINIEST THING WE EVER DECIDED TO PUT OUR WHOLE LIFE INTO...

Rahul and Mallvika looked forward to the joy of raising Neer and the unique experiences that come with it. They were totally engrossed in loving, holding, touching, watching, smelling, and playing with Neer. They learned parenthood by gaining knowledge from doctors, expert members of the family, and quite often from the mistakes they made. They soon became experts in knowing the problems that the baby goes through. Neer was a happy baby and hardly cried; the only time she cried was due to some health issues.

Rahul had a lovely voice and used to sing NAVKAR MANTRA as a lullaby for Neer," The Ṇamōkāra mantra or Navkar Mantra is the most significant mantra in Jainism and one of the oldest mantras in continuous practice. This is the first prayer recited by the Jains while meditating." And soon, it was Neer's favourite lullaby, and she was so used to it that even if someone missed singing, she used to hum herself until they sang.

Neer had turned two months, and it was time for their visit to Nana's place. Mallvika and Neer had come to her mom's house, and Rahul accompanied them most of the days as he couldn't go without any of the two. Suryakant and Jasumati were enjoying the best time of their life. Spending time with your grandchild is a totally different feeling; nothing can come close to it. Suryakant was enjoying the most; whenever he was home, he couldn't separate himself from Neer. He used to talk non-stop with her as though she could understand every bit of what he said; he used to make her learn sitting by stuffing pillows all over her; he also made her sleep by tapping her back, and Neer, too, was very comfortable with her nanaji.

It was the first wedding anniversary, yes Rahul and Mallvika had completed a year together as husband and wife but it was like they had been together from ages. Even though it was their first wedding anniversary they had been together for fifty-two months now.

They couldn't plan a trip as Neer was just two months old, so Rahul could only plan for a candlelight dinner. The couplets were out for the first time after Neer's birth; it was like a completely new experience. They couldn't come out of the parenting zone as their heart and minds kept repeatedly reminding them of Neer until they had called and checked if all was fine with her, and they were at peace after sharing the contact details of the restaurant in case of an emergency.

Rahul and Mallvika could now see and feel each other's presence as a couple and realised the atmosphere was lovely; everything around looked splendid in the dim light, the soft live music was so pleasing, the breeze was soft and pleasant, the table was on the edge of the pool and the moist in the wind was so romantic, the candles on the table made everything look beautiful and above all Mallvika looked ravishingly stunning in the black saree, the post-pregnancy had left a special glow on her face.

They reminisce about their days of secret meetings, especially on the terrace staircase, the movie date, the meetings at Naresh's house, the long drive on a rainy day, the college meet, and the day spent together in Ahmedabad.....it was like they lived their courtship days again. Rahul had not forgotten to get the chocolates and the rose for his beloved. Rahul and Mallvika were at their best; they had no complaints, were happy about all good things happening, and were extremely glad about sorting out the unpleasant things happening in their life. They felt no complaints, only gratitude for the good in their lives and contentment in overcoming past challenges. Rahul was so thankful to the DESTINY for giving him everything that he wanted. Mallvika was also happy that their struggles had very well paid off.

They prayed for the continuation of their golden era. After a lovely evening, they returned home feeling blessed.

It was time for Mallvika and Neer to go back home. Suryakant and Jasumati were feeling very sad about it, but being in the same city, they were happy that the connection would continue. Suryakant and Jasumati had given everything that, as per rituals, was to be given at the time of the wedding. To Mallvika, they gave all that was given in the bridal trousseau, and to Rahul as their son-in-law, gifts to all the close family members of Tolias were also given, as they couldn't arrange it while the wedding took place. Other than this, gifts were given in abundance to Neer from their maternal grandparents, including baby clothes, jewellery, cradles, prams, bouncers, walkers, toys, bath essentials, etc.

It's usually said and believed that the entry of a daughter in the family will boost the family with happiness and prosperity.

Neer's entry had also not only boosted Rahul's business but the family was soon moving from rental to their penthouse. Everything was going well. The relationship between the family members was getting stronger.

Neer became a reason for a smile on every face. Neer was a happy, clean, and active baby, and she kept everyone busy with her cute smile and her actions. Neer's cradle during the day was kept in the living room, and she was swung by every member passing by her side.

She had been showing regular changes in her sleep pattern, but on the nights when she was awake, she used to play with Rahul and watch and listen to the song "MUKAABLA" on VCR; it soon became her favourite song.

Days passed by, Neer was like a toy for the family. She was running at every corner of the house in her walker, kept shifting from room to room entertaining one and all. Mallvika and Riddhi used to gently throw Neer at each other over the bed, it used to take away Reena's breath but the little active baby Neer used to not only love such stunts, but enjoyed it the most and reacted with a loud and non-stop giggling.

Neer was a very friendly child and never hesitated to go to anyone. She always accompanied Rahul and Mallvika for all the outings on Sundays, but Suryakant insisted, they leave Neer whenever they went for a movie, especially on Sundays, as he could spend most of his time with her.

As Neer was five months old, Rahul and Mallvika with Neer started planning their weekend trip with their friends, as before. Most of the trips were planned spontaneously. Rahul and Ranish used to suddenly call from the office to get things packed for two days, and by the time they reached home, Mallvika and Rupali, with both Neer and Saloni (Ranish's nineteen-month-old baby), were ready for the trip. These spontaneous trips became some of the most memorable moments of their lives, rekindling their connection with friends.

From their first smile to their first steps and beyond, every milestone achieved fills your heart with joy. As a parent, you have a front-row seat to the miraculous process of your child's physical, emotional, and intellectual development, which is both humbling and awe-inspiring.

CHAPTER 15

Today's Moments are Tomorrow's Memories....

When everything in life is good, we don't realise how quickly time passes. Rahul and Mallvika felt the same way, caught up in the happiness and contentment of their lives.

Moments are the blocks that build memories, and these memories make up our lives. Rahul and Mallvika also experienced the small and large events that shaped them into who they were. Some moments are joyful, some are sad. But every moment, regardless of its significance, has the potential to become a cherished memory.

In the Tolia family things were changing. There were disagreements on authorities and powers, and unequal treatments among the members had ruptured the growing bond. Some of them choose to be silent whereas few opposed. It was like the spark had ignited but had not yet lit the fire. But it had definitely created a conflict atmosphere.

It was time for Tolias to move to the new house. Everyone was ready to pack their stuff, and a sudden announcement was made. Chetan had made a decision to get separated from a joint family; he said: "Reena and I are not moving to the new house; we will continue staying here and soon will book another flat and shift there." It was a shock for everyone, but nothing really changed as it looked like it was pre-planned; it was decided that others would move to the new house.

The family was growing, and Ripun and Riddhi soon shared the news of a new member arriving in the family. Once again, the family had moments of happiness.

The family had shifted, and it was time for unpacking. Mallvika and Riddhi had started arranging things, and there was another shocking hint from Riddhi; she passed a message by telling Mallvika, "Joint family will not last too long, soon you will also need to move from here, so its sensible not to unpack all your stuff" Mallvika was shocked and was trying to understand what exactly she meant, it looked like after Reena now it was her turn. Mallvika did not react; she just shared it with Rahul as there was nothing hidden or secret between the two. The two could sense things were not right, but Rahul, as usual, preferred to be silent as he was never considered by the family for any kind of decisions, and moreover, he had never questioned the family. Mallvika always respected Rahul's thoughts and kept silent.

Rahul was excited, as it was Mallvika's birthday. No trip was planned as the shifting and setting up was going on, yet Rahul had planned for a dinner date as that could be managed. Rahul had purchased a small gold pendant set, like the one he got for Diwali, with all-time favourite chocolates and roses. The couple had grabbed two hours from the hectic schedule and had a blissful time together. Rahul gave the gifts, and Mallvika appreciated them. They had a good time together and were back home. The love between the two was growing with every day that passed by.

The next day in the office, Vinesh and Chetan spoke to Rahul," Rahul, we are in a joint family, and everyone should be treated equally; we don't approve any acts that could cause problems in the family, so the personal gift that you gave to Mallvika is not appreciated. In the future, there should not be any such acts from your side." Rahul was dumbstruck and badly hurt. Rahul very well understood the joint family scenario and was also aware of how equivalently the members were treated. It was nineteen months since they got married, and the family had not yet given Mallvika the jewellery and outfits that they gave to Reena and Riddhi during their wedding, so Rahul tried to compensate for this inequality by giving small gifts even though Mallvika had no complaint about the same. Rahul felt suppressed as usual, as he always chose not to argue with the family and kept silent. Moreover, this time, it was not a mark but a scar on his heart.

He shared everything with Mallvika, asking for an apology as he would not be able to give her anything in the future. Rahul felt very guilty about it and said, "My nature of being silent had made you go through a hell of experience before marriage, and I thought I would compensate for all that, but see, I am again choosing to be helpless; I am extremely sorry for it" Mallvika definitely felt bad and was hurt, but it was towards Rahul's heartbroken and not the gift. Rahul was her weakness; she consoled him by saying," Rahul, what matters to me is your companionship. That's my best gift ever, and I have told you materialistic things do not give me any happiness if it is paid for by the tears or pain in your eyes." Mallvika hugged Rahul tight and wanted to take all the pain he was going through.

True love goes beyond merely being heard; it's about feeling that your feelings are understood and holds importance for your partner," this feeling indicates emotional connection, trust, and vulnerability. True love feels less like anxiousness and more like the sense of calm that you experience after receiving a much-needed hug.

Neer was just a ten-month-old baby, but for her age, she was a very active and fast learner. She was ahead in all her childhood milestones, whether it be sitting, speaking, walking... She had learned the "NAVKAR MANTRA" and used to recite it well; she also grabbed a lot of nursery rhymes with actions. She was very fond of dancing and couldn't sit once the music was on, and if the garba songs were played, she would not miss taking her dandiya sticks; it was like full-on entertainment for the family. "MUKAABLA" was still her favourite song.

Rahul kept himself updated on upcoming technologies. Rahul and Mallvika wanted to treasure these moments because they wanted to share them with Neer when she grew up. We also need to remember to reassure them that they will survive these moments forever, so Rahul and Ranish purchased the upcoming gadget of that era, a Handy Cam. Rahul and Mallvika had not missed on capturing any of these unforgettable moments.

They had not only captured these precious moments but also recorded her whole day's routine right from the way she woke up from her bed, saying good morning with her cute little hands-on her forehead, saluting the morning with a smile, yes she always woke up with a smile on her face, followed by the full day activity and the way she ended her day and fall asleep by playing and rolling around the bed, all was captured. Rahul had practiced a routine to record all Neer's activities every Sunday, from her waking up to her pool time on their terrace to her Rasgarba with chaniya choli to her toy and rhyme time.

Neer was a year old now, and it was the princess's first birthday. Rahul and Mallvika had thrown a party and had invited all their well-wishers. Baby at this age hardly understood birthdays, but our princess was so excited about her birthday that she kept dancing to the tunes, jumping and raising her hands exactly with the beats, and with a huge smile on her face. The birthday was a blast; friends had made the party worth it.

Rahul had been doing well in his business with few defaulters, as every business has, but Rahul's approach towards it was not positive, and he felt guilty; he thought he was adding liability to the family. Mallvika used to make him realise that if the loss was a liability, then when he has good earnings and profits, he is adding assets to the family. In such cases, why is he not feeling proud and positive? But nothing could change Rahul's mindset. Rahul wanted to work harder, and so Rahul was motivated to start a part-time business on weekends when share trading was off. He ventured into chemical distribution and got many orders. Unfortunately, the manufacturer couldn't keep up with the demand, and the business had to shut down. Despite this setback, Rahul was happy with the experience he gained.

This time, Rahul had planned a trip for their second wedding anniversary. The trio with Ranish, Rupali and Saloni were out for a week. The trip was always awesome with friends. It always de-stress the environment and brings new life within you.

The Tolia family was blessed with a new member, Viddhi, an angel sent to bring happiness. Viddhi was born in Rajkot, and after two months, it was time for her to come home. Riddhi and little princess Viddhi received a warm welcome. Everyone was delighted, but the most excited was Neer. She took on the role of the elder sister with enthusiasm, mirroring all the love, pampering, care, and affection she had received. Neer was overjoyed about being an elder sister and often spoke cutely to Viddhi, saying, "Viddhi, see your didi is here."

As days passed, the bond between Neer and Viddhi grew stronger. Neer loved looking after her younger sister, ensuring she was always cared for and loved. The sight of the two sisters bonding brought immense joy to everyone in the family.

CHAPTER 16

Silence was Taken for Granted

Rahul's business was doing well, but things with his family were not so good.

Head of the family is about being present as a leader. It's about setting the direction for your family and running it with all hands joined. It's also about treating them equally, resolving issues and conflicts when they arise. When a leader isn't carrying out these critical duties, chaos reigns.

Within a span of a year in the new house, there was an unsaid separation under the same roof; things were getting ugly. Rahul and Mallvika were facing suppressive actions at all levels, financially, emotionally, and administratively. It was like the Gujarati saying goes," BOLE TENA BOR VECHAAY," which means the one who speaks will be heard... Silence was not given a reward; instead, it was taken for granted. Regular episodes of suppression had damaged the self-esteem of the duos.

It's said that romantic love is real and genuine, but only as an initial visionary stage of intimate connection while Rahul and Mallvika were getting matured, and so was their love.

Moreover neither the disputes nor the maturity stole the romance between them.

Mallvika had always let go and stood by Rahul when it came to materialistic things. But things were changing, now the self-respect of the duos was torn up, and she couldn't take these attacks. Rahul's silence was now hurting Mallvika, although she couldn't choose to leave his side.

Instead Mallvika preferred to convey the problems to Ranjula with the aspiration of unify, she had no intention of playing blame game but the motive was to get things right, and being young if they were at any fault then they could correct themselves. Nevertheless, no action was taken to solve the issues, it was totally unheard and unspoken.

Rahul was still in favour of being silent. He was confident the elders will definitely find out a solution one day and this thought of Rahul's was bothering Mallvika.

A perfect relationship doesn't exist, you have to work on it and make one happen. Holding to each other during the ups and downs is the key factor. Exactly this happened between the twosome, Rahul kept the romance alive and Mallvika lifted up the relationship with her non-stop support.

When Neer was twenty months old, she developed a wheezing issue that troubled her for two to three days at a time. It became very difficult for her to breathe, especially in a sleeping position. Rahul and Mallvika would hold her in their arms for long periods so that Neer could sleep peacefully. This repeated episode occurred every fifteen days.

The couple took special care of Neer, focusing all their attention on her treatment. Life changed significantly as Neer needed to be kept away from any kind of pollution. Even though Neer's health was improving, the paediatrician explained them that the cure would be time-consuming and require a proper lifestyle. Rahul and Mallvika dedicatedly started following the remedies suggested. They were confident that together, they would succeed soon.

Even though the bonds between the elders were shaken up, there was a strong connection building up with the kids. The parents also showed no discrimination between Neer and Viddhi; all showered equal love and affection on both. Rahul and Mallvika had continued the Sunday recordings, which were more fun now, as Neer had Viddhi by her side. They were having fun playing with toys, dancing, and enjoying pool time. The time spent with the kids was awesome.

The Vora family was growing, too, and there was also an entry of an angel in the family. Kalpesh and Rishita were blessed with a princess, and they named her "Shriti."

As the days went by, the clouds of blind beliefs were also passing by; the sky was getting clearer and brighter, and one could see the real picture.

Rahul, too, could see the real scenario; in the past few years, Rahul and Mallvika had noticed but had not bothered until it came upon their child. They could see that members have their individual savings. It had hit hard when they taunted Mallvika for not taking responsibility for their child and throwing it on Vinesh. They were too young to understand the politics played within the family and realised it when they noticed the equation of a joint family was solved with different formulas, and no single common formula was practiced.

During that era joint families worked by the head of the family who collected all members' income and looked after all expenses of all the family members equally.

Rahul had practiced the same and so passed all his income to the family kitty. He had not kept anything by his side, which he thought was the rule of a joint family, and believed all the members were practicing it. As per his knowledge, all incomes go in, and Pappa takes care of all the expenses of all family members equally, so he could never personally take responsibility for Mallvika and Neer, but soon he realised the indifference shown among the members for satisfying even their basic needs.

Despite good earnings, Rahul couldn't take responsibility for Mallvika and Neer; eventually, due to this reason, they also avoided opting for a second baby, which they so very wished for.

The indifference was very hard to digest, and it was more difficult for Rahul to puke it out, as neither his emotions were understood nor he was given the opportunity to voice out his feelings, and this has left a strong impact that now keeping silence had become his nature which even though he wish to, he couldn't overcome.

But things were different now; Mallvika's approach toward Rahul's silence was not wholeheartedly supported. She had happily braced his nature of unvoiced whether it was about the pending wedding gifts, or the daily basic financial needs which she managed from the gifts she got from her family, or the most difficult was to go through the hammering on their self-respect, but this time it was about their daughter Neer and indifference with her was not acceptable as it's totally their responsibility to take a stand for their child being parents. Mallvika, for the first time, was hurt and had her arguments with Rahul for still being unvoiced, but although she had heartburn, she was not able to fight, as her love for Rahul never allowed her to stand against Rahul in any situation.

This was the first anguished argument Mallvika had against Rahul since they were together. Will these affect their relationship, or will the twosome as always cross this path of disagreements while holding hands and hearts full of love?

 Destiny and Karma: Hand in Hand

CHAPTER 17

Suppression Leads to Frustration

The brain controls all the human organs, but this was not true in the case of the twosome.

When it was about the mind game, the duos were at the opposite ends but their heart had always overpowered the brain and kept them and their love intact. The fresh wounds couldn't shake the pillar of love although the indifference was unblemished.

For Mallvika, these heartburns were getting deeper since she was not given the treatment it actually required. Mallvika's subconscious mind couldn't get over it, and this resulted in repeated nightmares. Mallvika often had dreams of falling from a height..... Rahul leaves her alone......crying in deep emotional pain.... and feeling suffocated by being locked in a box. Her dreams were so reflexive that Rahul used to wake up by her weeping and the jerks of her body; he couldn't see the pain on her face and used to wake her up to relieve her from the trauma she was going through. Rahul tried very hard to free Mallvika from these nightmares by taking care of Mallvika with an extra gesture of love and care, as he knew

Mallvika was not wrong. Rahul's constant approach worked like glue to keep up the love between the two, although there was no freedom from the nightmares.

Kalpesh and Rishita were settled in Ahmedabad. There was again good news for the family, Rishita was expecting her second child. Jasumati kept travelling between the two cities to manage both sides, as Shriti was too young. Dhiraj was doing his MBA in Ahmedabad and Suryakant was also busy winding up his business in Madras so as to proceed to Ahmedabad.

Soon the Vora's fully migrated to Ahmedabad with the entry of the baby boy in the family. Kalpesh and Rishita had named the cute little boy, "Shruvil."

Although things were going well, Mallvika and Rahul were not able to come out from the discrimination behaviour as things were adding up, and no sign of justice could be hoped for. During this shady period, few things kept the twosome motivated: the strong bond and the extreme love they had for each other, Neer's presence in their life like God's unlimited blessings, Rahul's business, and their friends who lit the flames of joy. The time spent with their friends made them happy and lightened their hearts.

Chetan and Reena had also moved to the new duplex flat after rejecting the flat first they had purchased as they disliked it and wanted a better option. The new house after a few years proved lucky, the couple was blessed with the most awaited happiness of their life, Reena was expecting. All the prayers and the treatments practiced past thirteen years were paid off. They were blessed with a cute little princess, named Nemishi.

It looked like it was time for families to get bigger; there was an entry of a new member in the Vora family, too. Dhiraj's wedding was fixed with Rejal, and it was time for the wedding preparations. Finally, Tolias had arranged the balance ornaments for Mallvika, which was supposed to be given at her wedding, which was pending for the past seven years. The wedding was a grand success and the celebration was talk of the town.

In the span of two years, Dhiraj and Rejal were also blessed with a cute little princess; they named her Rushi.

Rahul always worked hard and wanted to grab every opportunity that came his way. After trying his luck in chemical distribution, he now had an opportunity to get an added experience in distribution of musical cassettes and compact disc (CD). He was very happy with his share trading business, but with the introduction of computers he had adequate time and preferred to utilise it rather than wasting it.

The only thing that bothered Rahul was the unfair gestures, which looked like they had no end. This was now adversely affecting Mallvika; she was transmitting from a jovial person to more of a frustrated person. Nowadays, she gets angry about simple things, and her nightmares appear too often, giving her restless nights, which leaves Rahul scared and guilty. Rahul

I had patiently waited for things to change, but nothing much happened. Finally, he had to give it up, as the silence was giving unbearable pain, especially to Mallvika and was also ruining their relationship. Rahul could sense that if things continued, then one day, everything would be destroyed. At the same time, he was also worried for Vinesh as, for the past few years, his health has not been good due to the stress he had after his loss in the financial broking business handled by Chetan and Vinesh, so he was afraid to talk about separation as it could lead to further stress. But staying under the same roof with disunity, inequality, and disrespect for the past nine years was destroying all the relationships. Finally, he grabbed a good chance and spoke to Vinesh, "Pappa staying in the same house with no sign of togetherness makes no sense, and it will be better if we separate before it gets worse and nasty." He continued with a tone of request, "We are still young to handle things on our own and will be happy and blessed if you stay with us." Vinesh replied with a normal and cool tone, "We were waiting for this separation for many years, now that you have said we will start looking for a house, and regarding us coming with you is not possible as this is my first house and I DON'T WISH TO LEAVE THIS HOUSE UNTIL I DIE." Rahul was extremely hurt by Vinesh's readiness and cool reaction towards separation and more for not accepting to stay with them.

It was like the injustice was not going to leave Rahul and Mallvika. The hunt for a house was on, and so was

 Destiny and Karma: Hand in Hand

the inequality. The two houses purchased for the elder brothers were a penthouse and a duplex flat, but there was no such sign while looking for the third house. There was no choice given to the twosome, and a regular three bhk was finalised. The duos were hammered repeatedly; the family totally ignored the pain the duos were going through. Rahul felt so helpless as the pain givers were their own family members, and his inner conscience never allowed him to stand against them. Rahul had no other option than to console Mallvika to move forward with whatever had been decided. Mallvika was definitely heartbroken with the injustice but at the same time was happier to move away from the daily torture, and her focus was on life, where she would at least have no complaints and frustration for Rahul being silent, as these quarrels between the duos were very painful.

The past few years were very depressing for Mallvika, and this depression, humiliation, and suppression drastically changed Mallvika's nature.

Moreover her heart was never willing to but her frustration came out in the form of quarrels between the twosome and she was not at all liking it. Rahul could understand Mallvika's behaviour and felt guilty about it as it was because of him being non-vocal, Mallvika had to go through all these.

Love can be a feeling and a choice at the same time. Love often leads to physiological changes in the brain, but you can still decide whether love ends or lasts. Choosing to lean in and work through conflict with your partner may show that you are choosing to love rather than abandon the connection.

Even though life had spread more of thrones than roses, the twosome were still on the path of love, walking and holding hands, right from their teenage love to the journey after their wedding.

 Destiny and Karma: Hand in Hand

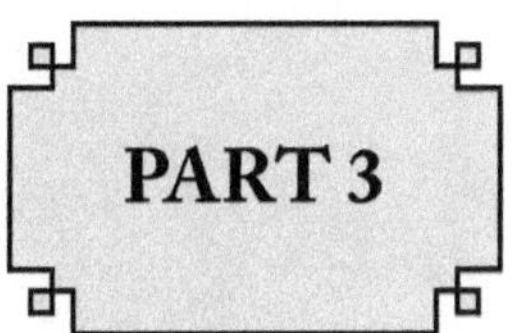

Was it teens or was it forties,

It was always a beginning, and not the
ending....

Was it destiny or was it karma,

That kept them bonded with all the
trauma...

Was it life or was it death

The couplets will never

Seperate....

CHAPTER 18

Home Sweet Home

A HOUSE IS BUILT WITH BRICKS AND BEAMS.
A HOME IS BUILT WITH LOVE AND DREAMS
A HOUSE IS WHERE THE HEART CHEERS....
A HOME IS WHERE WE ALL ARE REAL.

When we think of home, we don't just think of a house. We think of all the things within our house that make us feel cosy, warm, and loved.

Finally, it was time to move to a new house, their home. Even though twosome were not going to get freedom from the inequality and suppression as the houses were separated and not the family kitty, the practice of financial activities was going to be the same. Yet Rahul and Mallvika were happy and looked forward in positivity as they always did and promised themselves that their home will be free from humiliation, suffocation, disrespectful behaviours and will have no scarcity in love, respect, freedom and most importantly equality among the triad.

Our happy home has a foundation of love, walls of support, a roof of trust, and a floor of equality among the trinity.

Every corner of the house was designed and decorated with mutual choices and selection by all three; yes, Neer was only ten years old but was part of every decision made. One of the main reasons for involving Neer was Rahul's feelings of suppression, as he was not involved in any decisions made as he was the youngest, and so he was not ready to pass this suppression behaviour on to Neer. Rahul wanted Neer to grow as an independent and confident girl capable of making her own decisions. The trios had designed the house with their own expertise.

Soon, the house had turned into a home where every corner was filled with happiness and prosperity. Rahul and Mallvika were feeling so blissful, and their teenage romance was back. The sweet custom of "farewell and welcoming" was still intact and dedicatedly followed by the duos; in fact, there was an addition to it. The new house was on the third floor, and the balcony faced the roadside; the morning farewell at the door was conveyed by saying, "Mallu hu jau chu" (Mallu I am leaving) and was continued by Mallvika with an extra gesture of goodbye from the balcony and Rahul looking upward from his vehicle on the road, this was the routine that was followed forever.

Rahul was doing very well in his business, both share trading and cassettes & CD distribution, but he was not happy as even after good earnings he couldn't look after his both darlings and they had to face the financial indifferences, and this kept hurting him.

The Honda Group had bifurcation; there were many entries as everyone got married and had kids, but now as the group had more numbers, it was split into a few small groups, and our split new group had Naresh & Khyati, Ranish & Rupali, Keyur & Neeti, Yusuf & Ameena, Veeraj & Esha and a new entry Nipul & Fejal, with all the kids. The group was closely attached and was more like a family. Our house had become an ADDA. The group had a routine of going to a movie every Friday or Saturday night and for dinner and beach on Sundays, and this had become their routine. In addition to this, they used to spend one Sunday of every month from dawn to dusk at the "ADDA." They continued their regular weekend trips, but now, they were with the whole group and not only Ranish and Rupali. Everyone was bonded so well and had been the support pillars to each other during their tough time. Nothing was secret between them; they shared good and bad and always guided each other towards the right path. The group got its name "BONDS" from the strong bond they had between them, and of course, one of the reasons was "James Bond" fans.

It was time for Diwali, and the new house had a new ritual setup for their non-blood family. The Bonds used to celebrate Diwali Pooja with their families, and then all gathered at the

ADDA for their type of celebration with the people they have chosen to be part of their lives. The bonds used to burst crackers on the terrace and stayed till late, having snacks, desserts, and non-stop fun. Not only Diwali but Valentine's Day and New Years were also celebrated together every year in our home sweet home.

Every house where love abides
And friendship is a guest,
It is surely home and home sweet home.
From there, the heart can rest.

As the poet Nida Fazil said
Kabhi kisi ko mukammal jahaan nahin miltaa
Kahin zamin to kahin aasamaan nahin milta..
(no one ever finds perfection....... Sometimes you don't get land and sometimes you don't get sky.)

Everything was more than good; Rahul and Mallvika only had economic confines and inequality issues from the family side, but other than that, they were free from all stress and were actually living the life that they had always dreamt of.

The couplets were extremely happy with what they had, and with their positive approach, they kept going in life.

Rahul and Mallvika were dedicatedly involved in training Neer; it was their top priority.

Neer's upbringing had made her a person full of love, care, and respect for others. She was a lively child and always kept smiling. She was par matured to her age and a well-behaved girl. Neer was very attached to Viddhi, as they had grown up together, and the separation had not separated them in any manner. In fact, Viddhi, most Sundays, accompanied Neer to the restaurants and beach. Neer was also very fond of her maternal cousins, Shriti, Shruvil, and Rushi. Even though they only met during vacations, they had a great bond between them.

Mallvika was totally in charge of educationally training Neer; she looked after all her studies and extracurricular activities. Neer was doing well in all the parameters. She was a talented girl; she excelled in her academics and did excellent in other curriculum activities, too. Due to her wheezing issue, Mallvika took her to sports activities daily for two hours. She actively participated in roller skates and basketball tournaments. She had a very good control over her literature skills as she had developed reading at a very early age. She often won Geeta chanting, storytelling, and poetry recitation competitions. Neer's all-time favourite activity was dancing. Rahul and Mallvika were very proud of Neer.

Life with friends was awesome, the time spent with Bonds was always like a booster. No stress, no worries and no ifs and buts...it's only fun and great pleasure. There was a new craze in the group, the only males had started to go yearly once for a trip for two days. They used to enjoy the trip as they recalled their childhood days.

Whenever Rahul went for these trips, Mallvika couldn't stay alone, she had Phobia of being alone and especially she couldn't sleep alone. She tried hard but couldn't overcome the fear of sleeping alone and so Neer used to accompany her while Rahul was not in town.

Even though everything was good and Mallvika was enjoying every moment of their life, her nightmares were still with her; she was not finding any rescue from them. But the sudden entry of "SAI BABA" in her life had given her peace. Rahul and Mallvika had never ever worshipped "SAI," but one night, Mallvika had a dream of "SAI," saying," I am here to take all your pain and will walk with you through all the paths of joy and sorrow. I am here to hold your hand and walk by your side forever." Mallvika and Rahul were religious but not a core follower, but the dream had a different impact on them as they had never before heard much about "SAI" and had never followed or gone to any "SAI" temple, and failed to interpret the meaning of the dream or reason of its appearance, as usually it's believed that we dream of those things of which our mind is constantly occupied with but there was no such case here.

As days passed, Mallvika occasionally felt "SAI's" presence in her regular activities, but nothing much could be acknowledged; yes, Mallvika started feeling peaceful and followed a routine of chanting his name as it gave her relief and peace from the inner frustration that had bottled up. The duos commenced their regular visit to Sai Temple on Thursday evenings. Rahul had been regularly practicing visits to the Jalaram temple every Thursday morning and, on the way back, used to do "Annadanam," offering food packs to the needy, with Keyur and Nipul.

The blissful days were on and the trios were at their best, it was like the prayers, the good deeds and their dedication were paid off.

For a long time, Rahul and Mallvika have been planning their second child, but due to the stress they prolonged, they now feel it is time to proceed. Twosome always wanted two kids, but the situation had not been favoured. Now, as the duos were free from daily stress and could proceed toward their wish for the second baby, they were a bit confused about the age gap between the kids. After thinking for a long time, Rahul, with his own experience, felt," Mallu, I think we are too late; Neer is ten now, and siblings with a long age gap will never be a company," so they gave up on their wish for a second baby. The trios soon learned to be happy with the family of three.

Having a place to go is a home. Having someone to love is a family. Having both is a blessing. Rahul and Mallvika felt blessed.

CHAPTER 19

In the Middle of Every Difficulty Lies an Opportunity...

Rahul and Mallvika were going through the healing phase of their life. All the wounds during their past struggles were healed through the joy and happiness they experienced in their home with no sign of disunity, inequality, or disrespect.

Life is full of unexpected challenges, but we must always keep in mind that every challenge we face only makes us stronger.

The couplet's have become stronger with every hurdle they passed. It was time for a new pain in their life.

Vora's family came to know about Suryakant's disease; he was diagnosed with cancer. Mallvika couldn't keep her strong as fighting against problems and against disease are two different things. In this difficult phase, Rahul boosted her positivity and gave her strength.

Mallvika often visited Ahmedabad to look after her father, and Rahul, in every manner, very well supported Mallvika. Whether it was taking care of Neer, home, or the emotional pain of her father's disease. Rahul took over everything very well.

During this difficult time there was a news that brought smile on every face, yes there was good news in the Vora family, which gave them moments of joy. Dhiraj and Rejal were blessed with an angel, and she was named Riya, their second daughter. Suryakant had a great time with the newborn. He kept himself busy with his regular routine and also went on trips with Jasumati. He very gracefully lived his life by spending it with his loved ones. He patiently fought his disease with no complaints.

He tried to fulfil the aspirations he had in his life; one of them was to follow the traditional ritual of KANYADAAN, which he couldn't do for her only daughter. But as it's said, "It's never too late," his wish was accomplished, and Mallvika's KANYADAAN Pooja was performed; it was like a mini wedding of the duos.

After two years of fighting, cancer had won, and Mallvika lost her father. However strong we are, losing our dear ones breaks us apart.

Rahul always showed extra gestures of love and care in difficult situations. Soon life was getting back to its routine but missing our dear ones always stays in our heart.

Due to advanced technology there was no scope left for cassettes and compact disc, so Rahul had to shut down his business. Everything in our life leaves us with more knowledge and experience even if it doesn't succeed. Nothing goes to waste, Rahul had not only earned profits but had also gained wisdom, experience and contacts.

Neer, at the age of fifteen was aspirated and had commenced her religious fasting "AATHAAI" fast for 8 days. In Jainism Aathaai means going on a only water fast for all eight days and on the ninth day the fast is released, the sugar candy water and mung water are the first drinks offered that too spoon by spoon. This breakfast meal is a called "PARANA" and it's celebrated with all family, friends and relatives who come together to feed.

In the past, in the Tolia family, this fasting was done by Rahul, Mallvika, and Reena; in fact, Reena had done it twice, and all these were grandly celebrated. Now it was time for the PARANA celebration of Neer.

On discussion, Chetan suggested not to have a grand celebration; instead, only the first family members would get together to feed Neer. It was a really heartbreaking experience for the duos, especially for Rahul. Never in his dreams had he thought of such partiality, which he couldn't take, and he reacted on the spot with disappointment," Bhaiyla, Neer is just fifteen, and at this young age, she has fasted; I think every member should be enthusiastic about this celebration. How could even one think of no celebration." The power in Rahul's voice was totally different; it was the first time Rahul had voiced his feelings, and that too with no questions of ifs and buts. It's believed that a parent can do anything for their kids, and this was the proof, the first time at the age of 38, he had chosen not to be silent.

The Parana was celebrated well. All the family members, friends, and relatives were part of it.

Rahul's business had shown good growth, but at present, had faced some losses. However, every span of five to seven years, Rahul faced a loss due to defaulters or in personal trading, which is normal for any business. But Rahul felt guilty about these losses, thinking they were a burden on the family. Mallvika would often explain to him that just as profits add assets to the family, losses are part of the business cycle and shouldn't make him feel low, but he was culpable. He felt he was passing the trouble of debts to his family. He never considered passing of all the time profits that he gained, but the passing of his rare loss bothered him a lot.

Every businessman has to face ups and downs; everyone in the family had their part in profits and losses, but Rahul was not okay with this. He wanted to take responsibility for his acts, and so he decided to detach himself from financial activities. Mallvika and Rahul had come to Vinesh's house, and Rahul spoke to Vinesh," Pappa, from now onwards, I would like to take responsibility for my losses and don't feel right to pass it in the family kitty, and so from hereupon I will manage my profits and loss, I would like not to bother you people for any of my debts or expenses, indeed will not give or take any money from the family."

The family was not okay with it; things were not easy, and there were a lot of conflicts on the detachment. All members had their views, and the discussion was on. All of a sudden, the needle was turned to Mallvika; she was blamed for the loss. Some of the family members had accused Mallvika by saying, "You must have pressurised Rahul for funds, and that's why he has faced this loss." Mallvika was stunned and speechless; she was here to support and stand by Rahul as he was feeling so very guilty about the loss; he kept blaming himself and always failed to express himself well, and in such a situation, Mallvika was not ready to leave him alone, as she knew Rahul needed her the most, but instead, she was accused and proven guilty. Mallvika was shocked and felt so very heartbroken; she had been accepting all the partiality and inequality from the day she got into the Tolia family. She had never been taken care of, even her basic financial needs, which she managed from the gifts she got from her parents. She had not voiced out for her rights as a daughter-in-law even though she was given things in the span of 7 years, and today, she is blamed for money.

Mallvika had been disrespected in various ways since she got married, but she took it all just because she was madly in love with Rahul. Even though her heart had forgiven every punch, her mind had a mark of unsupportive behaviour of Rahul, but she had never allowed her mind to win over her heart. Today, Mallvika's eyes were only on Rahul, hoping to take her stand while she was showered with the splash of blame from the family members. Rahul, too, was shocked and shattered as for no reason Mallvika was blamed, but by the time he could voice his support, things became nasty. Mallvika couldn't take those few seconds of silence from Rahul and left with disappointment. She was badly hurt by the family but more so because of Rahul's silence. She thought, like always, Rahul would take no action to support her.

On the other end, before Rahul could say anything, Mallvika reacted, but he knew what Mallvika was going through, so he, instead of consoling Mallvika, felt it was more important to take the right stand for her. Rahul responded to the arrows of blame thrown on Mallvika. Rahul explained to his family members," Mallvika had never ever asked for anything; in fact, she has only given from the day she was connected to me and always stood by my side holding my hands with her support, and materialistic things had never mattered to her, in fact, what mattered to her was her self-respect and that too she has ruptured because of me. Regarding this loss, why is it that Mallvika is being blamed, even though if there was any profit, it was to be added to the family kitty and not given to Mallvika? She was here to support me, and nothing more mattered to her. Saying this, Rahul left; he wanted to apologise to Mallvika for all that had happened.

Mallvika was back home and hugged Neer tightly to reduce her pain. She wanted to calm down but her frustration which had bottled up the past 16 years had erupted. Rahul too was home and tried talking to Mallvika but she was totally broken and was not in state for any conversation. Rahul hugged her tight and consoled her with unspoken words. Soon Mallvika calmed down and there was silence for a long time.

True love means accepting each other's imperfections and loving the whole person with all his flaws. It's a more grounded and realistic view of each other.

Tolias was not happy with it but agreed to it in their way of not sharing and dividing the savings earned to date. Rahul and Mallvika asked no questions and had started from zero. They choose to be unarticulated about any kind of conversation regarding the savings and earnings of Rahul's past 18 years. Henceforth it was an unsaid decision that all past savings will be under the family kitty and Rahul will start with zero.

Aristotle was the first to suggest that everything happens for a reason. He believed that everything happening to you today has a purpose as it helps you to become who you are and for what you are in this world.

EVERYTHING HAPPENS FOR A REASON.THAT REASON CAUSES CHANGE. SOMETIMES IT HURTS. SOMETIMES IT'S HARD. BUT IN THE END IT'S ALL FOR THE BEST.

CHAPTER 20

Blessings in Disguise

Difficulties exist to be surmounted....

There is some greater purpose or meaning for what has happened which is determined by fate, a higher power, God.

Rahul and Mallvika were also unable to crack the reason behind the partial separation, but in the long-term, they will understand the real purpose behind this act.

Nothing had changed between the core love they shared at teens and now in their forties other than the added maturity and responsibilities, in fact their love grew with every disagreement, conflicts, arguments and fights.

Mallvika, who couldn't stay away from Rahul, had soon forgotten the pain she went through, and the duo were back again like teenage lovers. They were ready to take up their new challenge with their all-time favourite weapon," love," which had not dwindled in any situation.

The twosome had a few days of hardship as they were dealing with the restart of their savings. But in the span of a few months things were smooth as Rahul always worked hard, his dedication and efforts had soon got them into a better position.

Mallvika was still trapped with the nightmare which had no sign of relief, but her Sai chanting had helped her and made her more calm and composed.

Rahul, after shutting his cassettes and compact disc distribution, had now conjoined with Dhiraj, who was in the manufacturing of cycle tubes. Rahul had taken marketing of the tubes for Tamil Nadu. Rahul had always engrossed himself in working hard, utilising every minute, and never hesitating to try new things. This business required a lot of travelling. Rahul often left on Friday evening after his trading and was back by Saturday night as on Sunday; he wanted to spend his time with Mallvika and Neer and, of course, bonds. As Mallvika still had the Phobia of being alone, Neer continued to accompany her while Rahul was not in town.

Things were falling into place. Rahul was doing well in both his businesses, and soon, they had commenced on savings. They started their regular lifestyle. It was like a "BLESSINGS IN DISGUISE "; Rahul, who always chose to be silent, had voiced out for separation due to the guilt he felt for the loss he made, and this, in turn, has given them the opportunity to take over their financial activities and responsibilities. It was after 16 years of their marriage that Rahul had actually become amenable to his family's responsibility, and he felt extremely happy about it, as he knew, at least from now on, they could plan and execute their thoughts and desires toward their future and, most importantly, Neer's future.

Mallvika's most of the time had been utilised in looking after and mentoring Neer. Right from beginning till 8th grade, Mallvika looked after Neer's studies and no other coaching was required but now it was time to train her to be self-efficient and so Mallvika started guiding her to study on her own, soon Neer had taken over and could manage on her own.

Now Mallvika had ample time as she was free from Neer's coaching, and this extra free time bothered her a lot. Thinking of past events, she was heading towards depression. As the saying goes, "An empty mind is the devil's workshop."

Rahul decided and took care of it not to happen. Rahul soon realised and encouraged her to do something that would keep her occupied and, most importantly, happy. Mallvika appreciated the idea but was thinking of a part-time job

      Destiny and Karma: Hand in Hand

as her priority was Rahul and Neer, and she wanted to be always available for them. After a few ideas and discussion, Neer and Rahul suggested her to join pre-school as a teacher to the toddlers as Mallvika loved spending time with kids, and she had a good command of training them. Mallvika, too, was interested but was not confident enough about her performance as a teacher. The kiddos need a lot of diligence, and with her changing nature, she doubted if she could keep her patience. Mallvika's personality will not allow her to do something unless she is confident about it. Her nature of "not quitting once involved" was still the same, so she chose to qualify herself for the work she wanted to start. Mallvika got into post-graduation in "Early Childhood Education," which was a one-year course. She did well and started enjoying spending time with the toddlers; it was like a stress reliever. She got her degree and joined a pre-school as a teacher.

Human life is an endless interplay of joy and sorrow. Just as a coin has two sides with heads and tails, a person's life has two different sides which are completely opposite to each other.

Rahul always worked very hard and had always dreamt of early retirement. Rahul wanted to work only till the day he saved sufficient capital to look after their expenses and aspirations. Now, it was time for Rahul to work towards it.

He had started planning on the estimation of all his future requirements, and as per the needs, he had his strategies ready for the accumulation of capital and the various ways to invest them in safe, secured, and best-yielding plans. His journey towards it was on, and he was glad that Mallvika was with her on this journey, too, leaving behind all that had discommoded her.

Soon, things were fine. Life was back on track. Rahul was doing well and started executing his savings plan. He not only wanted to secure the future but also wanted to gift Mallvika all that he couldn't do in the past, but now Mallvika felt it was inappropriate, and she explained to Rahul," Rahul, I am happy that you want to give me all that you wished and we both awaited all these years for this moment, but now we are parents first, and our top most priority is Neer and her needs. She is fifteen, a grown-up girl, and soon we will need funds for her higher education and wedding, so first, let's secure all her requirements and our future needs. I have waited so long, and I am quite patient enough to wait." Rahul had kept Neer's requirements on top, but he also wanted to give equal importance to Mallvika.

The twosome decided to rework on their priorities list, the series was Neer's education, Neer's wedding, health and basic requirements, trips and retirement needs......

Rahul and Mallvika believed in making memories and that's the reason Rahul always initiated get-togethers with loved ones. He always planned and executed a movie night and a dinner, at least weekly once with the "Bonds" and at least monthly one lunch with family, and this became a core routine. Everything was going well, they were not aware but they were really building strong memories for the future.

Neer was doing excellent in her academics. She had cleared her 10th grade with par excellence, and it was time for her to choose the course. Rahul encouraged Neer to opt for commerce, keeping chartered accountancy in mind as Neer could get close guidelines from Ripun being a chartered accountant, but there was no compulsion, and Neer had full liberty to choose her career. Neer was more inclined towards biology and hence chose the pure science group, not with a very clear idea about which stream to opt for in the future. But Rahul and Mallvika we're gearing up as it was sure she would choose a major career, and in such case, Rahul wanted to be ready with the funds that may be required, and Mallvika was ready to be by her side for any kind of encouragement, motivation and support she may need.

Neer was in her 12th grade and had faced severe drug allergies; she got rashes and swelling all over her body, and soon she started feeling compression on her lungs and couldn't breathe. It was serious; Mallvika contacted one of Neer's classmate's mother, who was a dermatologist and explained the situation. Dr. Renuka immediately suggested bringing her home as it was midnight. Rahul, Mallvika, and Keyur took Neer to Dr. Renuka; she gave her emergency treatment and also informed her hospital to keep the emergency care unit ready; if in case the treatment she gave did not work, then Neer was to be shifted there. Within an hour, Neer felt better, and things were in control. Soon, she started recovering, but the past two hours were like hell for the duos; they were thankful to Sai and Dr. Renuka, who was no less than God to them. Neer was very inspired by Dr. Renuka and the profession, which gave a different feeling of achievement of saving someone's life, such a noble profession. The incident influenced Neer toward the medical profession, but yet was not sure or confident about it. She was inspired by the thought that in her lifetime, if she could even save one life, she would feel worthy.

Neer had cleared her 12th boards with flying colours especially in her core subject, biology. It was time for her to confirm her inclination towards the medical profession. Being biology as a major she could think of any medical field but Neer was interested in doing MBBS. As there was no medical career background in the family, she was a bit confused and felt difficult to decide on what should be done.

                Destiny and Karma: Hand in Hand

The trio had met and spoke to a few doctors in the family and friends and had lots of discussion specially with Ripun, Dhiraj and Keyur who had their expertise on education and the education system.

Finally, after gathering all the information, clearing all her queries, and after a lot of discussion, Neer chose to get into MBBS. As it was not pre-planned, Neer had not prepared for NEET, the entrance exam for medicine. Henceforth, there were two options left: either take a break for a year, prepare well for NEET, and score high to get into a government college where the fees will be very nominal, or prepare for a month and, with the score achieved, get into a good private college where there will be a huge fee to be paid.

The discussion also revolved around the family, and Vinesh was not happy about Neer getting into medicine; he had worries about a difficult career that would take a long time and have a huge fee structure. Being a grandparent, he was also worried about Neer's wedding; according to him, if Neer opted for medical, then it would be too late for her wedding, and it would also be difficult to spend both on her fees and her wedding. But Rahul was clear on that ground and explained to Vinesh," Pappa, don't worry, by God's grace everything will be managed, and even if there is any shortage, will prefer not to spend on the wedding, but no compromise will be made on the education front. Daughters need to be independent, and education is the key to this."

With the blessings of Sai, Rahul managed his financial activities well, and in the span of three years, he accumulated a good amount of savings and also managed their basic to luxury needs well.

Taking a break for a year to prepare for NEET was not favoured by any members as it was a prolonged course of five and half years plus the specialisation for three years, and adding one more year to it made no sense. Now Neer had two choices: either to get her admission in Gujarat, an hour from Ahmedabad, or in Chennai. Admission in Gujarat would cost half the cost in Chennai, which would be convenient for Rahul, but Chennai was her hometown, and it would be more convenient for Neer to be with family. So, there was a bit of confusion about finalising the centre. Dhiraj had explained to Rahul and Mallvika, "Medical will not be easy to crack, and during her course, she will go through a lot of difficulties, and you both, being her side, will give her support and security to move ahead so as not to think much and let's finalise on Chennai," at the end Neer's convenience was given more important and admission was taken in Chennai.

Dhiraj played the role of a counsellor, Ripun was like an adherent and Keyur was involved in all the admission procedure, all beside the trio, was like a booster.

Rahul struggled but managed with his three years of savings and a small part of his investments. Tolias and Vora's were not okay with breaking any form of investment; instead, they suggest to take a loan, but Rahul was not okay with it as he couldn't work under pressure of repayment, and that's why he preferred not to take any kind of loan neither from the bank nor from both the families. He knew the expenses of upcoming years would be high as every year fees and savings for specialisation and weddings were also ahead, so he was not ready for the added pressure of repayment. It was not only in this case but Rahul always preferred and, in his lifetime, had never chosen to take loan for any of his requirements.

As we look back on our life, we realise that every time we thought we were being rejected from something good, we were actually being redirected to something better."..

Rahul was so very pleased with his recent decision of taking hold on his income as in the previous scenario he would have been helpless as definitely this huge expense would have been rejected and he would have failed in building up Neer's future.

"Everything happens for a reason,"

The phrase conveys the belief that the events and experiences in our lives are not haphazard. Instead, they have an underlying purpose or cause, suggesting they shape us into who we were born to be.

Trio's struggles were not over, and so was their determination. Rahul was busy with the achievement of future requirements, Mallvika was busy with her new venture, and Neer was working very hard towards her profession as she wanted to do her best to prove that the belief and freedom she was given were worth it and above all she knew her parents have stood against many odds to let her pursue her dream career, even though Rahul and Mallvika had kept door open of quitting the course for Neer as they knew it's going to be hell difficult to achieve success and they wanted Neer to be free from any kind of pressure or burden. Eventually, with all their busy schedules, the trios never missed the family time and kept the relationship intact with love and affection between them. The bond between the trios was getting stronger and stronger.

It was time for Neer's first year result. The trios were all crossed fingers, hoping for the best as somewhere, each one had its own battle towards its victory. God had planned their life full of struggle but also had given them strength and the urge to fight and win the battle, and the trio won this, too. Rahul was the most excited, thrilled, and overwhelmed. He couldn't control his happiness, and the happy tears poured

 Destiny and Karma: Hand in Hand

down from his eyes. It was a proud moment for the trios. The trios shared their proud moment with friends and family, and a special vote of thanks was given to Dhiraj, Ripun, and Keyur for being on their side and guiding the path.

The whole kit and caboodle was going well. It looked like it was the best time of their life. With every struggle we face and overcome, we feel happier than the previous achievement; Rahul and Mallvika also experienced the same. After every battle, they experience the best time of their life; nothing could be better than this.

It was time for a trip for the Bonds and this time it was not a weekend but the kids strongly insisted on an international trip. It was the first international trip for the duos but Neer had joined Kalpesh and family for an international trip before. All bonds were part of it and it was the most memorable trip.

There was a new entry in the family; Shruvil had come to Chennai for his engineering. He used to be home every weekend and during holidays. It was like the dream of a second child was fulfilled. Neer and Shruvil were very fond of each other, and Neer was blessed with her wish to have siblings. They had a lovely time together. Rahul enjoyed his company, and soon, they both shared the father-son relationship. Mallvika was the only parental aunt, and she always pampered all the kids and had a good bond with one and all. Shruvil and Mallvika got even closer. It was like a dream come true. Rahul, Neer, and Shruvil used to team up and never missed a chance to pull Mallvika's leg. The family could feel a sense of completion with Shruvil's entry.

Rahul," Fortune favours the brave.' our destiny claims for a very hard work but then we are always blessed with whatever we dream of, Sai has fulfilled our dream of second child in form of Shruvil."

Mallvika replies," Sai is always with good soul and you are not only good but a very kind soul who can never intentionally hurt anyone." Mallvika continues with mischievous tone," apart from me, as all the pain is always in my plate." The couplets had always uplifted their life by finding joy in little moments.

Neer was in her third year now. She needed to spend more time on her studies, so it was decided that she should shift to the hostel, which would save her 3 hours of travelling every day. Neer's migration to the hostel was not taken well by Mallvika as she missed her a lot even though both Neer and Shruvil were home every weekend. Mallvika's nightmares were intacted and added to her restlessness. Rahul could

     Destiny and Karma: Hand in Hand

feel the uneasiness Mallvika was going through; he started taking care of her emotional stress by spending more time with her. They again started going for morning walks, and in the evening, Mallvika used to walk down to Sai temple, and Rahul, on his return back, picked her up from the temple. They most often had dinners on their way back home. The couplets enjoyed this new phase of their life.

From the age of 16 to 40, nothing has changed between the two; their personality and their emotions for each other still has the fragrance of a rose and the sweetness of chocolates.

CHAPTER 21

Frenemy

Destiny had decided to test the couplets in the time span of almost every five years. Every time the duos fought, thinking this will be the last one, there pops up a new challenge tougher than the previous one,

It looks like there was no end to it.

For the past seven years, Rahul kept working hard and accumulated savings in various investments, but now it was time for the wheel of fortune to turn around, as life is a combination of good and bad, and nothing is permanent. First the distribution of cycle tubes had to be closed down due to some manufacturing complications and then there was a loss in share trading business as a result of person trading.

Habitually, Rahul started self-accusing, and his guilt bothered him so much. He was in utter desolation and couldn't think ahead; this time, Mallvika didn't take it lightly, and she decided to find a solution to it; she gave a choice to Rahul: "Rahul, you need to take a call on what exactly you want. If you indulge in personal trading, then you need to accept the losses too; you can't only have profits on your plate. Either you take up the loss just the way you embrace the profits or quit personal trading and from now on concentrate on the brokerage." Rahul could understand what Mallvika said, and he knew she was right. Mallvika continued," Rahul, this time, you have to take a call among one of these as it's very difficult to see you going through this stress. We can happily survive with less money, but more money with stress is not acceptable." Rahul also knew it was high time to take a final call on it, even though personal trading gave him ample profits. Loss gave him unmanageable stress, and in such cases, he was not capable of taking any decision, and things got even worse. Above that, he knew his brokerage was more than sufficient for survival; eventually, he decided to quit personal trading. Rahul spoke to Mallvika,"

MALLU, I FEEL I SHOULD QUIT PERSONAL TRADING AS IT MAKES ME INDECISIVE AND I MAY RUIN EVERYTHING, SO I PROMISE YOU AND NEER I WILL NOT INDULGE IN PERSONAL TRADING FROM NOW ONWARDS."

Mallvika was happy with his decision. Rahul was his weakness, and she couldn't see him unhappy or stressed.

The duos now had to concentrate on the present situation and had to arrange funds to cover the loss. They had invested their recent savings in various fixed investments, and they did not wish to break them midway as it was meant for Neer's education and wedding.

Rahul and Mallvika were thinking of various ways to solve the situation. Mallvika had suggested getting funds on a loan, but persistently, Rahul did not encourage the idea of taking a loan. Moreover, a thought had troubled Rahul since few months, when one of his neighbours suddenly demise at a very early age. This scared him, and he realised everything was so uncertain, and if something such happened to him, then what would happen to Mallvika and Neer? It's his duty to secure their future; he can't trust or depend on anyone, not even on his family, to take responsibility.

Hence he decided to get his share of savings past 25 years from the family kitty as it was high time to take his financial activities in his hands and organise it as per their upcoming needs so as to secure his family's future. Mallvika was stunned but was also happy that finally Rahul thought of being assertive. She invariably stood by Rahul in his decision.

Maybe this loss was a sign from God as Rahul only voices out when something is utmost required just like the episode that happened seven years back.

Rahul had spoken to family members regarding the requirement for his share of savings. After much discussion, the family decided to give only the amount required to repay the loss, and the rest will be continued in the family kitty. Rahul was not okay with it, and this time, he wanted to get his complete share as he now wanted to seek out and plan all his savings against his requirements to know where he stood and what exactly his requirements were. To date he was just moving ahead with no clarity of what he has and what he requires, but now, at the age of 45, he should secure his family as life is very unpredictable, and in such cases, Mallvika and Neer will be in trouble even after his hard earnings. Moreover, he didn't wish to continue any kind of financial connection as it was leading to quarrels and conflicts.

On Rahul's request, the family finally agreed and sent just a figure with no calculation, no explanation, or no clarification. Rahul was shocked and felt the figure was inappropriate, but he wanted to end this conflict, so he accepted whatever they had decided by saying," Pappa, I was disappointed as I thought I should have been part of the calculations, but as usual I have not been considered, and the figure you have confirmed seems to be discriminatory as per my understanding, and if I am wrong, please correct me. I feel sorry for my blind trust in my family, and at this point, I realise my silence has been taken for granted, yet I don't want to get into any arguments, and I abide by your decision."

Things didn't go well; it was like a huge, nasty volcano erupted. There was blame, abuse, hatred, and whatnot.... Rahul couldn't understand the response he got as he had just shared his feelings of injustice towards the accounting of his share they had derived, yet he had already surrendered and accepted what was decided by them without asking any further questions then why was this reaction, if the family felt he was wrong than they could have pointed out the same and explained him where was he wrong. Instead, they choose to play the blame game.

Rahul was devastated, and finally, he chose to voice out his feelings, which had been suppressed all his life; he couldn't be vocal and chose to write a letter mentioning all that they went through in the past. He highlighted all the inequality, indifference, disunity, and disrespect...they had gone through without any rebellion, and the reward for their amenable pay was paid well. He also apologised by saying," If at any time in our lives, we were wrong and had hurt any of the family members, then we are sorry about it," but they had not received any kind of response from the family.

YOU HAVE THE RIGHT TO LEAVE SOMEONE, BUT AT LEAST LET THEM KNOW WHY BECAUSE THE ONLY THING WORSE THAN BEING ABANDONED IS KNOWING THAT YOU'RE NOT EVEN WORTH AN EXPLANATION.

Things didn't stop here; there was more to come...

Things did not end well, and wealth had finally overpowered the relationship. The Tolia family had disowned Rahul and his family by sending a letter of "NOC," which specified that Rahul and his family had been given their share, and from now onwards, they have no rights in any assets or capital that belongs to the Tolia family and so on...

Rahul, on receiving the letter, was totally broken; no words could explain what he felt. Mallvika tried hard, but nothing could console him; it was like Rahul had given up on his life and had no further interest in living. Mallvika was feeling helpless and couldn't understand how to retrieve him. She was not only helpless but very scared of his life-quitting behaviour, and she couldn't take it. Mallvika, at this moment, could only think of reverse psychology; she said," Rahul, everything is because of Neer and me; if we were not in your life, you would have no fights and would be free from all conflicts, so not you who needs to quit the life, it should be us." It worked, and Rahul's grief broke out in tears. Mallvika allowed him to lighten up, and she hugged him tight with the gesture of not allowing him to go anywhere. After some time, Mallvika questioned Rahul," Rahul, why is this NOC bothering you eminently? We have never raised our voices for any kind of inappropriate rights or shares. In fact, we had let go of what was ours. Then there is no question that we wish to claim something from theirs, so what is that that disturbed you so deeply?" Rahul replied with extreme pain in his voice," Mallu, that's what has hurt me exceedingly. What had made my family think this way? Where did I go wrong? The day I started earning, all my earnings were given to their hands with no questions, no expectations, and no queries. Seven years back, we had started from zero but had not claimed any share then, and today, at the age of 45, I asked for my share and the figure they derived, in my opinion, was unfair, yet I accepted it. I am a person who has compromised and left my share. Will a person like me claim someone else's share? Does my family think of me in this way? If my parents, who have brought up me think about me like this, then I am a big failure. I have no right to live in this world."

Mallvika could understand as not only Rahul, she was also badly hurt, but it was time for her to take action and she told," Rahul I understand but what others think is not in our hand, we need to be honest with ourselves, we know we can never claim any kind of share from family which is not ours so let's take it practically and sign this NOC and give it to the family once we receive all that the family has promised us as our share."

Rahul was so badly hurt that nothing could imperturbable him. He decided not to respond; in fact, he regretted unfolding his feelings; he said," Mallu, I felt my silence was not comprehended, so I was at fault for being unspoken. I had never told them what I was going through, so they couldn't apprehend and find solutions to the problems I faced, and that's the reason I chose to voice out this time with the hope of sorting everything out. I preferred to convey to them what was hurting me, but even then, they couldn't understand either my wounds or my intention, and everything was destroyed." Rahul took a pause and continued," Mallu, I am thankful to God for sending you and Neer in my life. I feel Sai has sent you as his shadow to take all my pain and give me peace, and Neer is like a blessing of all my good deeds, yet I don't protect you both; indeed, I take you for granted. I am so sorry."

Rahul's one out of the four priorities was out his "FAMILY."

Rahul, who had been quiet all his life just to keep up with the family, was totally broken down, and today, everything was destroyed. Neither Rahul nor Mallvika felt worth talking to

 Destiny and Karma: Hand in Hand

them, nor did the family show any gestures of continuity. In fact, few members chose to socialise the family matters on social media.

The two were hurt badly, and it became very difficult for them to cope with what had happened; the only thing going through their mind was after struggling and compromising all their life with the intention of keeping the relationship alive, today, they were standing with dead relations in their hands.

None of the two had left with the energy to console each other anymore, and for a few days, there was total silence, trying to come out from the disaster.

Unsaid love and affection between the two were helping them to overcome these difficult days.

The total connection with the family was broken, and there was no communication on any platform. The Tolia WhatsApp group was inactive for the past month, just like their life.

It was not the end of their exam; life had more papers coming up...

It was Viddhi's birthday, and the duos can never choose to cut down with kids. Mallvika had personally sent the birthday wishes message to Viddhi as for her, Viddhi was no less than Neer. But Rahul had messaged Viddhi on the Tolia WhatsApp group, and Mallvika did not take this well. She was very discomposed, and she expressed her disappointment by saying, "The family had abandoned us the past month, and especially how broken you were when we received the letter of "NOC." It took such pain to overcome those defamations. we had gone through so much humiliation, and they have not missed the chance of abusing us, yet what is it that still connects you to them." Mallvika was not only disappointed but also furious; she continued, "Rahul, you had always taken me for granted, but no more. I have always stood by you, and now it's your turn. To date, we have compromised with our self-respect, but in no circumstances am I going to encourage any such thing and demand the same from you. Despite such unethical behaviour from the family, you are still welcoming them; how could you? Don't you feel frustrated? How can a person be so forgiving?" Mallvika was totally shaken up by this act as she thought Rahul had learned his lesson and would no longer allow people to use him, but within a few days, Rahul was back, always available for people to allow them to take advantage of him. Thus, Mallvika decided to make Rahul realise the consequences of any such acts in the future by teaching him a lesson.

Mallvika, with all her anger and frustration, said," Rahul, you could have called Viddhi or messaged her personally; why was there a need for you to message in a group where you have been thrown out? Keep a little bit of attitude in your pocket; don't use it to hurt others, but at least use it when your self-respect is being tested by other people. Instead, you have always torn apart your and my self-respect, too, and heretofore, I always stood by you, but if we are not ready to change ourselves even after such drastic acts, then we can never learn our lesson. Today, I have lost hope in you, and I am sorry to say that even though I can't think of being away from you, I need to think about being with you as I have had enough and don't wish to hurt our feelings and respect anymore. Being with you makes me feel like I am a dustbin that is always available for people to throw any kind of behaviour at me. I am done with all this shit."

Rahul never, in his dream, thought of this day, could understand what Mallvika was going through, and he understood his mistake very well. He tried apologising, but he knew sorry could not heal the pain he had given. Rahul couldn't imagine his life without Mallvika, but at the same time, he felt he didn't deserve her." Mallvika had compromised at all levels and crumbled herself just to complete me, and I have always taken her for granted; she stood like a pillar for me against all odds, she healed all my wounds, she pampered me when I felt depressed, she became my mouthpiece whenever required and above all she boosted confidence in me which survived me till day, do I even deserve to say sorry to her. How could I convince her that I will change." But with all this in his mind, Rahul couldn't think of being away from Mallvika, so he chose to speak to her," Mallu, I don't even deserve to say sorry, and I know you will not believe me anymore; I don't have right to stop you from going away, but I am being selfish again and requesting you to forgive my acts, and please be my side as you always did." Mallvika," Rahul, I can't compromise on my values anymore to please others; I would now like to keep my self-respect intact and walk away from all these corrupted and fake worlds."

All the hard efforts of the lovebirds had gone in vain. The destiny played its role and the karma had to bow down. It looked like, in the fight between the DESTINY VS KARMA, karma was out beaten by destiny.

Finally, destiny had victory over karma.

Karma means your life is your making. Karmic accumulation can either be a Boost or a Burden, which is our choice.

That is so true; it's only our actions that lead us to Boost or Burden. The twosome's life was full of these examples. If in their teens, Rahul had not worked hard to prove himself capable and Mallvika would not have chosen to elope, they could never have been together; it was the BOOSTER of their life, and the same way if the duos would have chosen to protest against the indifferences they faced throughout their life than they would have never faced the BURDEN in their life.

Mallvika always believed in moving forward with the lessons learned from life at every stage.

Whether it was at the time of Rahul's back-off in her teens or now when the family ditched, she wants to move ahead instead of blaming either the person or the situation that caused us pain. She believes no person or situation can harm us until we allow them. We, by not protesting, give them permission to do whatever they want, and if it is bothering us and we feel it's not right, then we need to take control; if we don't protest or take over, it's a mistake from our side, no one else should be blamed.

In the past, Mallvika had allowed Rahul's acceptance of his family's wrong approach to her. Rahul meant much more than anything else, but today, she is not ready to allow any such things because of Rahul's respect; moreover, his existence is much higher than anything else. It was time for Mallvika to teach Rahul to keep the TRIOS above everything else.

Eventually, Mallvika decided to tell Rahul," Rahul, your action has distributed me to the core, and I need time to understand where Neer and I stand in your life. Even though you passionately love us, you have always taken us for granted, especially me, but not anymore. So, I need time to understand if there will be any change or if you will choose to run behind something that only gives you and us pain. In such a case, I don't prefer to continue, no matter how hard it would be for us to disconnect."

It's about mutual growth, support, respect, and understanding. Both partners are invested in each other's happiness and well-being.

Mallvika was in so much pain to say such things, but she needed to be strong as she wanted Rahul to understand the value of the right people in his life. She continued, "And only for this reason have I decided to go to Ahmedabad so I can think without any emotional pressure. At the same time,

I very well understand what you are going through, and as much as I need you, you need me too, in fact, even more, and I can't think of leaving you alone in this difficult situation. So Neer will not go back to the hostel; instead will stay with you." Rahul was shattered; it was like he was incapacitated to accept Mallvika's decision, and his guilt of disappointing Mallvika made him impotent to stop her. He was quiet, but his heart was screaming; he felt very restless and eagerly hunted for a solution, as the only thought of losing Mallvika was killing him inside. Eventually, he called Dhiraj and told him about everything that had happened. He then said, "Dhiraj, I know I am at fault, but I can't even imagine a day without Mallvika, spending life without her; oh no, how's that possible? She is my life." Rahul was in severe pain, and Dhiraj could feel his pain over the phone. Rahul continued," Dhiraj, I beg you to save my marriage, as without Mallvika, I don't exist. I know I have never valued her and always taken her for granted, yet she always kept herself available for me and stood by my side. I don't deserve her, but again, I am being selfish and only thinking about myself. I know that even though I extremely love Mallvika, I have not done justice to her; today, I want to promise you that in the next 25 years, I will compensate for all that I missed. Dhiraj, please help me." Dhiraj consoled Rahul and said," I am coming there tonight and will find the best solution, and believe me, things will be fine; till then, keep calm, and I will also talk to Mallvika not to think much and wait until my arrival."

Rahul and Mallvika were so very disturbed; in their entire lifetime, they were never so disconnected; both wanted to communicate and share the pain, but none had the courage to talk, yet their eyes could exchange the pain they were going through.

Dhiraj had reached Chennai, Keyur and Ranish also had come home. On their arrival, the duo explained the situation, and Rahul said sorry for his altruistic behaviour. He felt guilty about how easily he made himself available to everyone.

On the other end, Mallvika expressed how badly she was hurt by his self-degradation. Mallvika said, "After all that happened, he should respect himself enough to walk away from anything that no longer serves him, grows him, or makes him happy. By now, he should learn that the way he treats himself sets the standard for others on how he demands to be treated. He shouldn't settle for anything less than RESPECT. If he keeps carrying this behaviour, it's impossible for me to stay by his side. I can never hate him or get disconnected from him, but at the same time, I am not ready or available anymore for any kind of disrespect from anyone."

Dhiraj, Keyur, and Ranish had tried with their way of explanation. Dhiraj spoke to both Rahul and Mallvika in his way. He explained, "You both need to be isolated from each other for a few days as both have been hurt badly by the unexpected and unpleasant incident that occurred, and if you continue together, you both will ruin your beautiful, loving relationship, as now you people only have pain, frustration, anxiety, dismay and apprehensive to share with each other. None of you are in a position to take care of the other; in fact, you both need to be taken care of. I strongly suggest you both come to Ahmedabad for a few days as it will change the environment, and you people can restart with fresh minds." Keyur and Ranish agreed to it, but Rahul was not comfortable with it. Dhiraj then spoke to Rahul in private and promised him," Rahul, believe me, let Mallvika come with me for a few days, and I am sure she will forget all this and will be soon back to you if she still feels the same, then I promise I will convince her, but I am very sure it will not be required. It's only a matter of a few days. And I still prefer you to come with us as you equally need to retrieve." Rahul could understand and agree with his solution, but he preferred to be in Chennai.

On the other end, Dhiraj spoke to Mallvika," Mallvika, come with me to Ahmedabad for a few days; when you feel a bit composed, come back, and everything will be more than fine. You both being each other's side, nothing can go wrong." Mallvika instantly reacted," No, Dhiraj, I can't even think of leaving Rahul alone in this situation; yes, I had definitely told him that I want space, but it's only for him to change his behaviour. I want him to start respecting himself; if he doesn't respect himself, no one else will. To date, I have compromised just because he did all this for his family, but his family had just thrown him like an outsider, so no more attacks on either his or my self-respect. I know at this moment when his family has disowned him, his eyes are stuck on me, and I equally need and want to be with him as I too feel very depressed, and Rahul is the only anti-stress medicine for me." Dhiraj knew Mallvika had taken this step just so Rahul could understand the worst situation possible. Dhiraj could understand Mallvika very well, but he could see beyond, and so said," Mallvika, I very well understand your concern, but you need to understand that if you both want to be together as you were all these years, then this break is very much required, a partner can be helpful only if one of them is calm and composed but at present you both are hurt badly, and both need to be healed if in this situation you people chose to be together than your wounds will infect the other instead of healing. So believe me for once and come with me for at least a week." Mallvika could understand what Dhiraj meant, but her heart was not allowing her to leave Rahul and go. Finally, for the betterment of the two, Dhiraj convinced both, and Mallvika went with Dhiraj after giving strict instructions to Neer, Keyur, and Ranish to look after Rahul and not to leave him alone. Mallvika requested Keyur to take special care of him, and Keyur promised to call Rahul to his art gallery and work from there. Mallvika then spoke to Neer," Neer, you know how shattered daddy is; I know he needs me the most right now, but mamma (uncle) is also right; I am right now mentally weak and so not in the position to be his strength and after me I can only trust you, so please be with daddy all the time and take care of him." Neer replies, "Mumma, at present, you too need special care just like daddy needs, and I want to be with you too in this difficult period, but I feel secure as mamma, and the whole Vora family is there to take care of you and don't worry I will try my best to comfort daddy and will always be by his side but mumma, please come back soon." Mallvika," Neer I had not disclosed, involved or shared anything to anyone in Vora family all these years, and at present, Daddy had spoken to mamma and requested him to come, so for others in the family, I am just going for a casual vacation, yet I will be fine them being around me."

It was the toughest time in their life. None of them were okay with Mallvika going to Ahmedabad, but they knew it was obligatory. All three, with heavy hearts, said goodbye until we met next.

True love doesn't mean you will never break-up; it just means you will always get back together. Two people who are meant to be will always find a way back. They may take a while to find one another, but they are never lost.

Something that keeps people going during the worst times is "HOPE," and the trios also temporarily departed with the HOPE OF FOREVER TOGETHERNESS.

Mallvika physically left, but the soul couldn't...

TEARS AND RAIN
FALL DOWN ON FACE
MY BODY IS UNABLE TO STAY
YET MY HEART IS UNWILLING TO LEAVE.

CHAPTER 22

Silver Jubilee

TRUE LOVE IS ALWAYS THERE, AND IT WILL NEVER LEAVE...

Sometimes, our situation will keep repeating itself until we learn our lesson...

The two had now learned their lesson and were ready to move ahead with a new attitude toward life.

Often, individuals commit a lot of energy to put in the effort that a long-term relationship may require for its future and health.

Mallvika kept a check on Rahul's mental and physical health; she kept guiding Neer through the various ways of comforting Rahul. Mallvika and Rahul were restless and repeatedly kept calling each other. The conversations were very limited from Mallvika's side, but Rahul did not miss any chance and solicited a new start. He assured Mallvika that if given a chance, he would make sure there would be no regret or disappointment. Dhiraj spoke to the duos routinely and encouraged them.

No one can escape from the word "struggle" in their lives. We need to be a warrior to fight under any circumstances to conquer happiness. The duo's struggle too had its victory and it was a time of moments of joy.

Eventually it was time for the reunion of the lovebirds, Mallvika was back within a week. Gradually life was taking a turn towards the path where the most beautiful part of the duo's life was waiting.

Neer stayed home for a week as she wanted to see her parents just like before, madly in love with each other. Within a few days things were getting to normal.

Twosome got busy investing the share of the funds that they received. As the couplets had already worked on the requirements and investment plans, it did not take much time. All the future needs for the span of the next 30 years, right from their daily basic and luxury needs....their outings and trips......their medical and social expenses.....their casual and emergency requirements.....and most importantly, Neer's education and wedding, everything was computed, and the duration of the investment was also determined as per their time scheduled.

As of this date, the availability of funds was not adequate to match the requirement, but they were very confident that the upcoming savings and their investment plans would definitely yield enough to meet their requirements.

Rahul had always kept Mallvika aware of all financial activities, and all filing and accounting work was assigned to her; Rahul trained Mallvika as he wanted her to manage in all uncertain situations. In case of any uncertainty or emergency, she should be able to handle things independently. Rahul also wanted Neer to be part of it, but due to her studies, she couldn't spare much time. Thus, she was regularly briefed. Rahul's inner consciousness of the incident of the neighbour's death always scared him about some kind of uncertainty, and he wanted them to be ready to handle things on their own. Mallvika was not okay with this thought, and she initially ignored it, but then Rahul spoke to her about the fear he had," Mallu, I understand you are not able to accept the fact of unpredictability, but this is a bitter truth of life. I always wish and pray that we both take our last breath together after securing Neer's life, but it's all about destiny, which is not in our power. What is in our hands is to be prepared for any uncertainty as it's not only about us but, most importantly, it's about Neer. In case by any mishap I leave this world at any inappropriate time, I want to see you both safe and secure. most importantly, you both are self-dependent and for that, you need to know all about our savings and investments." Mallvika understood the practicality of the situation and commenced tracking all the financial activities.

Mallvika was feeling quite low from the day Neer had moved to the hostel; added to it, she was facing menopause, which added to her loneliness. There were numerous changes in her personality; one of them was feeling very lethargic and depressed. In this phase, Rahul gave her the best days of her life. He spent more time with her on a daily basis. He came home early, and they used to spend evenings on their terrace, talking about the day, gossiping, and listening to music. They went on outings like dinner, beach, movies, and long drives on almost every alternate day. Added to it, the lovebirds, with their friends, had gone on numerous domestic and international trips; Neer was hardly part of these trips due to her busy schedule with her studies.

Rahul very well took care of Mallvika, it was like a complete reversal of the past. The twosome were experiencing the best time of their life.

With the blessings of Sai, the couplets felt peace, and his presence helped the duos to again believe in forgiveness and forget. Sai had given them what they deserved and the life was awesome even after all the rocky road. Sai's preaching taught them that, anger makes a human smaller, while forgiveness forces you to grow beyond what you are. They realised that we should forgive others, not because they deserve forgiveness, but because we deserve peace. The couplets were now at peace and had eliminated all kinds of negativity towards the family from their side, even though there was only work-related communication. Many times, it's believed that either God or your sixth sense is aware of future incidents in the form of dreams, and it could be some kind of a sign. Mallvika's nightmares also could be such a sign, as for a few weeks, she had not gotten those dreams, and it could be a sign of their freedom from all kinds of pain, but Mallvika had no idea of its permanence or its dissipation.

Rahul was doing good in his business, and he found himself mentally peaceful at Keyur's Art Gallery. He started his daily routine at his art gallery and soon took over the management. All the spare time he had from his share trading business was spent at the gallery. After Rahul had promised Mallvika and Neer not to indulge in personal share trading, his extra business hours were peacefully spent there. He was very happy and relaxed, and so was Keyur, as he got a helping hand who looked after the gallery; now he had extra time and could think of business expansion. Keyur had offered Rahul his share in the profits, but Rahul had not accepted; he said," Keyur money can't buy the peace I am getting here and let it be that way." Keyur then compelled Mallvika, but her answer was the same. Keyur was not okay, and on his repeated request, Mallvika promised to take the share when Rahul started working full-time at the gallery.

Rahul's business was doing very well, and his expenses had been reduced as there were no more fees to be paid for Neer's MBBS as she was doing her internship. In the expenses list of the trios, Neer's fees were listed at the top, and now this was added to their savings. Within a short period, Rahul managed to invest the amount that was deficit as per their 30-year plan. Rahul felt secure as all the certain and uncertain expenses were invested. It was time for Rahul to do all that he wished to do for Mallvika all these years. Rahul gave a free hand to Mallvika to fulfil whatever she wished, from ornaments to outfits, gadgets to accessories, outings to trips. The duos were gratifying all their wishes.

The couplets were entering their 25th year of wedding. It was time to celebrate their Silver Jubilee. Twosome had planned a long international trip for only two of them. The duos were done with all their trip bookings, and on the other end, Neer had her own plans. She was secretly planning a proper wedding celebration of the duos. Neer shared her plans for the celebration with Dhiraj and Keyur for a double check. She had planned a grand celebration with all her friends, family, and close relatives. It was a proper wedding with a guest list of 125 pax. She had planned everything well, from giving personal invitations to organise all the events like mehndi and Haldi Sangeet to a felicitous wedding with all traditional rituals, as there were no rituals performed during their wedding.

Neer had spoken to the Tolia family to be part of the function, she had called her grandparents too, to come for the wedding, who were spending most of their time in their holy town. The Tolia family other than Vinesh and Ranjula had decided to be part of the functions.

The duos were on their trip. It was their first and only trip without friends and family after their honeymoon. The two had a wonderful time and enjoyed every moment. Mallvika was so very happy; she expressed herself," Rahul, these days are like the first few months of our relationship where we were totally immersed in each other, and we couldn't see or feel anything else other than love. Every gesture reminds me of all the first feelings we experienced then, and yet today, they feel so fresh and genuine. A day spent with you full of love resolves all the problems and pains and makes me feel eternal blessed." Rahul relevantly continues," Mallu, thank you for giving me one more chance, and I got the opportunity to fulfil all the dreams that I had seen for you and with you. Without you, the dreams would never be accomplished. I just want to compensate for all the difficulties I have had with days full of love. I am just waiting for Neer's getting into her specialisation and then for her wedding. Within two years, all will be done, and then we will enjoy our retirement, roam all around the world till the last day of our lives."

It was the end of the most memorable trip. The two had an excellent time and an unforgettable experience.

The couplets were back, and Keyur had come to pick them up; the duos were unaware of what Neer had planned. They reached home, but it was dark out; as they entered, Neer and Shruvil switched on the dim golden lights, and the couplets were surprised to see the living room was fully decorated with roses and all their photos from the past 25 years which were tied below the stringed balloons that were resting on the roof, the whole view was mesmerising. The duo had not yet finished looking at the pictures; there was another surprise: the whole Vora family, right from Jasumati to Riya, all suddenly jumped out from the bedroom, wishing them forever together; it was such a great pleasure to see them all. It was like the surprise was not going to end; Neer had kept outfits ready for the couplets and instructed them to get ready and come to the function hall of their apartment. As they entered the function hall, it was filled with Tolias and all other family members, relatives, and their favourite Bonds. It was an ecstatic moment for the duos. The family and friends had gathered for the mehendi ceremony. The mehendi artists applied mehendi to all the members and to Mallvika. Everything was so good: the music, the food, and the crowd, and there was dance and, of course, raas garba; gujrati's functions can't be completed without raas garba; everything was awesome and full of fun. Each and everyone had a blast. It was a late night, all were back home, and the most unexpected surprise was out. Neer and the family explained the events planned for the next day. Neer said, "Mumma and daddy, tomorrow morning we are leaving for the resort at 7 am; there will be the welcome ceremony on arrival at 8:30, then we will all check-in, and by 10 am is the Ganesh Pooja followed by Haldi and lunch. Barat welcome is at 4 pm and continues with wedding rituals by the seashore. After the wedding at 6 pm, there will be a blessing ceremony for the newly wedded couple. Later, the couple will have a formal meeting with all the guests. The dinner will be served from 7-9 pm." The two were looking at Neer, who, from their cute little princess, suddenly looked adult. She was always more mature for her age, but this responsibility was different. Neer took a pause and continued,

"To conclude, there will be a formal Sangeet, games, and DJ night, and once the DJ party is done, we all can rest as the check-out is on the next day after breakfast." The duos were shocked but were happy and thrilled seeing their daughter be so organised and responsible enough to manage such a big event. Rahul was worried about the expenses, but Dhiraj cooled him down by convincing him that everything was under control.

The next day, everything happened as planned, and all the functions were executed as per the traditional rituals. It was a lovely outdoor Haldi where each and all applied Haldi to the lovebirds; the food was awesome. It was time for the couple to get ready for the wedding. The wedding was well organised, and all the rituals were performed right from barat, jai mala, kanyadaan, hastmelap, pheras, mangal sutra, sindur… everything was followed in the proper traditional way. As it was a gathering of very close members, everyone was present for the Sangeet and games even though it was quite late. The kids of the family had excellent dance performances, and the event management team had well executed the games, which kept every age group involved. The event was a grand success, and it was marked as an unforgettable memory by every mind present there.

The two had enjoyed every moment and were so overwhelmed. They were extremely proud of Neer for initially completing her MBBS in one shot and now organising this wonderful wedding; it was like they had excelled in the parental test. They thanked Sai for blessing them with such a wonderful daughter.

Mallvika who had not strongly believed in rituals was suddenly trying to find a reason for all the rituals that took place at this stage of their life. She always believed in "every action has its reaction" and that belief of hers made her constantly think that there should be something behind this wedding, but what?

Patience is not the ability to wait but the ability to keep a good attitude while waiting. The couplets had kept patience with good attitude and even though their trials got harder and harder the rewards they received were marvellous just like the one they experienced now.

EVERYTHING COMES IN TIME TO THOSE WHO CAN WAIT......

CHAPTER 23

Pain and Pleasure.....

Rahul's priority list had one down, "his family." He had forgiven the pain, but he couldn't forget the betrayal, which is a very common human psychology. We move on, but the deep wounds leave some kind of side effects and are never totally healed. The duos experienced the same; they were back on talking terms, but the emotions could never be the same as before. They had learned to keep a distance so as not to get hurt again, but life is full of PAIN AND PLEASURE. We get hurt only by those whom we love the most.

Life had its role to play, and it was time for Rahul's second priority to fall. From his adolescent age, friends were his life. They were his mood changers; whatever life had given to Rahul, either joy or sorrow, every emotion was shared with his friends. They had always uplifted Rahul's anxieties just by being his side and had added to happy moments by celebrating it. But things were changing, something was going wrong within the group but was unidentified and unresolvable.

Any kind of relationship asks for maintenance; for better nourishment, we need to provide the right amount of time and respect and condone the behaviour. If we miss any of these, we start losing its value and importance, and the continuity of such an attitude will destroy everything. The same thing happened here: a few internal differences, a bit of arrogance, and some amount of just chill behaviour had loosened the threads of friendship, which resulted in a rift between the friends.

In a group, everyone has their own role, and Rahul's role was to keep everyone connected. He always took the initiative of making plans for their get-togethers, like going for movies, dinners, trips, or just gathering at one place and spending the day together. But nowadays, the plans were called off as the response from most of them was "no and not possible," it was like everyone either got busy in their life or they had started avoiding each other; the reason was not clear, but the emotions were losing their value.

For Rahul, friends were so important that this negative response pushed him towards loneliness; he couldn't think of losing his friendship. Mallvika tried hard, but she couldn't replace his friend. It looked like Rahul's second priority on his list was almost on the deathbed; there were few signs of its retrieval, and few of them wanted to work on them to get back to normal, but no required results were achieved; the only good thing was that their heart was still strongly connected even though they rarely met.

     Destiny and Karma: Hand in Hand

Mallvika who had got freedom from her nightmares was again caught with a different dream, this time she saw various forms of raising water like tsunami and flood, she saw Neer and herself being caught in middle of water and they had no space to escape. They were totally surrounded by water and nothing else could be seen. The restlessness of being trapped and the anxiety of saving Neer was the highlight of the dreams . This time there was no suffocation but it was only the obsession to somehow save Neer from being drowned. There were no sign of Rahul's presence in it. The nightmare was a repeated episode that disturbed Mallvika almost every 15 days. The dreams left her with the apprehension as it had not concluded whether Neer was saved, so the thought kept troubling her for long. Mallvika with her past experience was sure the dream had something to say and so she tried hard to interpret the meaning of the dream but the duos had failed, despite of consulting about it to the dream interpreters no satisfactory results were achieved. Mallvika used to read a lot of articles too but couldn't achieve any result.

★ ★ ★

It was Duo's anniversary, and Rahul, as usual, did not miss to plan a trip. Only two couples, Ranish and Nipul, were part of it; others couldn't make it. The two had a great time with their favourite people and at their favourite hill station; it was their 8th visit to this hill station. Rahul and Mallvika were happy to complete 25 years of their wedding and 28 years of their togetherness. Everything in life and around them had changed. The only thing stable was their selfless love and affection for each other. Even after decades, they enjoyed waking up early and going for a morning walk hand in hand; this gentle gesture was always appreciated and practiced by the two.

Life is like an ECG signal, full of ups and downs, which in both cases indicates that you are not dead.

The duo's life has also seen the peak, and so now it's turn for the fall.

Everything was going so well, but how is it possible that the love story of Rahul and Mallvika sails smoothly?

It was like life had decided to knock out the couplets. First family, then friends, the duos had not yet overcome the depression, there was another punch, due to the wrong trade; they had faced a loss. He couldn't take it as it's not easy to accept unwitting mistakes. When we knowingly or with our own desire do an act, and it proves to be wrong, we accept it as we have the readiness for it's happening, and so we acquire either by blaming ourselves or by taking responsibility, but it's very difficult to adopt a loss when you were not directly responsible, or you can say an act of destiny is not well accepted. In such cases, we are not left with an option of blaming anyone, and we also have no clue or answer, "How and why did this happen?" and this annoys us a lot. The same thing happened with Rahul; he closed all the doors to avoid any possibility of loss by filtering his client list and, most importantly, deciding on NO PERSONAL TRADING, but no one can win over destiny.

   Destiny and Karma: Hand in Hand

God moves in mysterious ways.

Go with the flow. Don't fight fate.

It is what it is. You can't fight fate.

It was always in the cards. It was fated

Mallvika as always tried to convince Rahul to move ahead as profit and loss are part of the business. Rahul was not ready to accept but was not left with any choice but to move ahead. He spoke to Mallvika," Mallu, I am really sorry I always drag you into the pit. I don't know what's wrong, but whenever we feel we are safe and secure and are at our best, we face the downfall." Mallvika sits beside him and tries to make him understand, Rahul's life is a mixture of ups and downs; we have to accept it with new hopes of a better tomorrow. And what you said is true but half true; everyone has their own perspective of looking at things; you see it as dragging into the pit, and I look at it as pulling out from the pit. I feel that if it's your act that gives us trouble or pain, then vice versa; it's only because of you that we are relieved from this pain or trouble. If because of you we suffer, then it is totally because of you we have all comforts, too, so stop thinking of all this and let us concentrate on how to proceed." Mallvika continued," Rahul, I still feel it's the right time for you to retire from this business as all our requirements are organised well, and early retirement was always your dream; above all, you have the opportunity at the age of forty-eight to get retire and enjoy life, and for this, you have worked so hard past 30 years. Rahul, it's not like you are going to sit at home all the time; you have a great option to go to Keyur's Art

Gallery, and you feel so comfortable there. And as you are not committed, we can always continue with the outings and trips you have planned." Rahul replied, "Mallu, you are right, but I want to continue till Neer gets into her specialisation as I don't want to compromise on it. I know we have already accumulated the funds required, but these are the only expenses for which we are not yet sure of exactly how much it will land to. I do agree we have arranged for such unexpected expenses, too, yet I feel I should retire only after her admission." Mallvika interrupts in between, "Rahul, I am not in favour of it and feel there is enough to fulfil all such extra expenses; it's the right time to stop here. I am not okay with unnecessary stress and guilt when we can choose to live in peace." Rahul was not convinced and chose to continue for another 6-12 months. Mallvika, even though was not in favour of it, agrees with Rahul.

The duos had as always sustained the loss and moved ahead. Soon they settled and things were falling on the right path.

Even though there were cracks in the friendship wall, Rahul and a few others tried to patch it. There was an international trip planned, and only a few of them could make it. Rahul and Mallvika were two-minded about going for the trip because of the stress due. to a recent loss, but the trip with friends always worked as a de-stress for Rahul, so the duos took this as an opportunity for a better change and continued the trip.

Trip with friends were always awesome, specially Rahul and Mallvika had spent lovely time together, a real unwind moment.

The duos were back, but the series of trips were not ending. It was like the couplets wanted to be away from all kinds of pressure and enjoy the beautiful life God had granted them. The duos had first decided to take a weekend trip for their anniversary, then there was a trip that Rahul had planned for a weekend outing with Bonds for friendship day, and after all this, there was a long international trip that Mallvika had planned for Jasumati. It was like the duos were on a tour, one after the other.

On the other end the recent loss was not getting out of Rahul's head and it kept him disturbed. His mind repeatedly told him to recover the loss by personal trading but his heart stopped him by reminding him the promise he had made to Mallvika and Neer of not to indulge anymore in any personal trading.

Rahul was wrestling hard between the mind and the heart. He kept reminding himself that there was no requirement for any compensation for the loss made, but his mind kept bothering him and subsequently increased his anxiety; he failed to understand why he was so restive. He also knew any action taken in this agitation will not give good results but yet he couldn't stop himself.

All through his life, he had chosen heart over his mind, but this time, the mind took victory over his heart, and Rahul had inclined towards personal trading. He somehow decided not to tell Mallvika until he recovered the fund he lost; it looked like this was not Rahul; something else was controlling him. He was into something that he had not done all his life, choosing to go against what his heart said, and, above all, the secret from Mallvika was totally unbelievable. His reactions were very different.

Rahul's market knowledge and favouring luck helped him to recover almost what he had lost recently. Rahul felt better and thanked God, "Thank you, Sai, for your blessings. I have come out of my mental trauma and am just waiting to get rid of a few more stocks, and then I will be done. The first thing I want to do is to talk and apologise to Mallu and Neer for breaking the promise I made, as it's hurting my inner consciousness. Once we are back from our anniversary weekend trip, I will tell Mallu everything; I know she will not appreciate it, and so will I. This looks like a repeat episode in my life in which I have been forced to do something that I don't believe in. First, it was during the courtship days when I gave up on life because I had to leave Mallu, and now, once again. The guilt of hiding these trades from Mallu, who credulously believes me, is bothering me so much; it reminds me of the day when I had broken up with her, yet she had not given up on me; she then trusted me blindly, and she now also trust me passionately, nothing has changed from her side and I have changed, it feels like I have actually betrayed her."

 Destiny and Karma: Hand in Hand

Mallvika, who knew Rahul so well, could figure out something was wrong with him. She sat beside and spoke to him, "Rahul, what's the matter? I thought a trip with friends would lighten you up, and during the trip, you were happy and relaxed, but in the past few days, I feel you are internally dealing with some kind of pressure. What is it?" Rahul felt deep remorse for being secretive despite Mallvika repeatedly demanding openness. He wished to confront, but he replied with guilt, "Mallu, the pressure is due to the volatility of the stock market and the clients who have been badly affected by it and nothing else. Don't worry. In a few days, things will be in control, and everything will be fine. "Rahul said what he believed deep inside was that things would be fine in a few days. Mallvika was not convinced, "Rahul, sure, nothing else is going on?" Rahul knew Mallvika would not believe so easily, so he tried to cogent emotionally and asked her to be calm as everything would be fine.

Mallvika was forced to believe as Rahul had never hidden anything from her all their life, added to it she was aware about the present fluctuations of the stock market. The frequent stressed conversation with the clients gave no reason to doubt yet her inner conscience was repeatedly telling her," Mallu something is definitely wrong, and so she decided to talk to him during their anniversary weekend trip."

It was the couple's 26th anniversary, and Rahul had planned a weekend trip for only two of them. The couplets were ready to go, but everything was different this time. The lovebirds were not as excited as they always are. Rahul was occupied with his guilt and pressure, whereas Mallvika was preparing herself to convince Rahul to quit business as she couldn't see him disquieting.

With a wish to leave behind all stress and worries, the lovebirds flew to the land of peace and love. As they started their journey they soon forgot everything and entered into the world of love where they could see and feel only each other's presence.

It was a dark, cloudy evening; everything looked so pleasant and nice; it was a perfect romantic evening out. As they drove, Rahul forgot all his fears and anxiety and could recall the first long drive of their life. He said," Mallu, don't you think history is repeating? Everything today is just like our first long drive; the weather is like a blessing from God, and the sight next to me is yet as ravishing as it was on that day; you still mesmerise me so much that I hardly notice the sight around me." Rahul paused and kept driving with one hand, and with the other, he held Mallvika's hand and gave a soft kiss on it, trying to say thank you for being mine, one of his favourite gestures towards Mallvika, he loved to hold her hand whether they were on a walk or on a bike ride or on a car drive. Everything was so perfect: the music, the weather, and most of all, the fact that his beloved was still sitting beside him, just like on day one.

                    Destiny and Karma: Hand in Hand

Mallvika, too, was lost in the moment. She was extremely happy to see Rahul back in his form," THE ROMANTIC RAHUL." When your beloved is happy, you feel all things around you are beautiful; Mallvika felt the same; everything was fantastic. The drive, the scenic view, the soft romantic music, and most importantly, the presence of the real Rahul beside her made everything feel so perfect. She glanced at Rahul, who was equally focused on her and the road and felt a wave of love wash over her. She still feels so complete being with him.

They had travelled about a few km from the city, had crossed the city traffic, and were heading towards the beach resort on the outskirts. The sight was so beautiful, the moment of the waves were so visible as the road was running parallel to the seashore. It was approx. A two-hour drive, but two were so very lost in the memories that they couldn't realise the time; it was like within a few moments, they reached the destination.

The couple had checked in and relaxed for an hour. The duo got ready for dinner. Rahul had organised a candlelight dinner by the shore. It was an awesome ambiance, with the dim candlelight, the sound of waves, and the fresh, moist wind; the sky looked beautiful with a few sparkling stars and the moon, and the soft instrumental music was perfect, just like the lovebirds. The two were complimenting each other. Mallvika, as usual, was looking simple and elegant in her black gown with her favourite accessories: the watch on her right wrist, a diamond bracelet, big diamond hoops, and her usual footwear, "flat pumps." She had the same natural" no makeup" look; the only changes that could be noticed were her short, soft, curly hair treated to straight midline length, the few fine lines, and the extra inches. Rahul's hair was still all over his forehead, and the salt n pepper look gave a dashing personality; with age and extra pounds, Rahul's plumpy face looked much cuter and smarter; his smile and the look he gave was so appealing, and it was still a moment of heartthrob for Mallvika. The couple had a lovely time and stayed on the shore until late.

Early in the morning, the couplets left for a walk on the shore. Everything looked so beautiful; the sun's thin rays glistened over the sparkling undulations of the ocean. The sunrise over the ocean is truly one of the most beautiful sights to watch.

There was a beautiful contrast between the blueness of the water and the whiteness of the sand. A cool breeze blows gently, adding to the serenity of an early morning walk along the shore. After a long walk, they sat by the shore. Mallvika was very happy with Rahul's approach, and he looked very calm and composed. There was no sign of tension, which Mallvika had felt the past few days. Yet as decided, Mallvika spoke to him," Rahul, for the past few days, you were so very tense and looked so worried, and it is very painful for me to see you so very jittery. I know we have already spoken about it, and as you said, it's all clientele-related pressure and stress, and I thoroughly believe you. But my concern is why there is a need for all these unpleasant moments. All these years, we have faced enough, and by Sai's grace, we don't need to go through this stress anymore." Mallvika parks her eyes on Rahul's eyes with a question, "Do you think it's not sufficient?" Rahul replies, "No, Mallu, I know it's more than sufficient, but with extra funds, we can have extra comforts of life. I just want to accomplish every little thing you both dream of." Mallvika came closer, rested her head on his shoulder, and proceeded with full of emotions," Rahul, there is no end to luxury; it's never enough unless and until we draw a line. For me, happy moments are more important than the surroundings; today, we can afford a candlelight dinner in a five-star resort, and our future plans have nothing less than this, so why do we need to be greedy? There is no end to desire, but we need to decide on what the cost is; I don't want anything at the cost of you being traumatised. I know it sounds so idealistic, but an anniversary with you," THE REAL ROMANTIC RAHUL," on our terrace means nothing less than celebrating at a five-star resort or equivalent. Rahul, you have been on medication for high blood pressure for the past four years, and this unwanted anxiety scared me a lot; I don't even want to think of it, but if this trauma turns into something worse, then what will happen to us? Please think about it. Our existence is the most important thing; everything else is just a momentary pleasure. We have planned and secured all our future requirements and needs, but our survival is even more important; we need to secure our lives." Rahul gave her a tight hug and expressed his feelings of being together forever with unspoken words.

Mallvika wished this moment would not end and they could be immersed in each other until their last breath.

Rahul always knew Mallvika's requirements, but still, he wished to do more than what he could. He started thinking of the secret trade and felt very guilty; he constantly cursed himself for hiding from a person who believed so much in him. He thought of telling Mallu everything right now, but yet something was stopping him from doing so. What and why was not understood. Definitely, DESTINY had some plans, "good or bad", only time will tell.

The duos were so very mesmerised among themselves that they perhaps were missing the signs that destiny was giving them in the form of dreams, restlessness, doubts, unusual behaviour... The lovebirds were unaware of the upcoming Tsunami, which would wash away everything and leave its devastating effects forever. Only time will tell what the couplet's destiny is.

EVERYTHING HAPPENS AT EXACTLY THE RIGHT MOMENT, NEITHER TOO SOON NOR TOO LATE.

The twosome had a really good time; in fact, this was one of their best anniversaries after the Silver Jubilee. The duos were back home. Mallvika was very happy about the way they spent their anniversary as she could be with the person whom she had loved since she was 16, and despite the numerous problems they faced, their love had not diminished. Rahul relished every second as he could forget all his stress and gathered the courage to make the decision not to withhold any more stocks and get freedom from the burden of uncertainty. He had finally decided to clear all his stock and book loss or profit the next morning as soon as the market opened.

Rahul was still a bit complex and scared of the share. He was still holding on. He hoped to safely come out of it and promised himself not to ever lose control and indulge in any such activity in the future. But destiny had some other plans. The stock market had crashed badly due to the announcement of the union budget. The market experienced a huge decline. Rahul was shattered; he felt he was trapped, and the shares he was holding had fallen to a great extent. He was so confused about whether to hold and wait for a better price or to sell off the stock and book the loss. Rahul was very confused and tried hard to find a solution. He was not ready to accept losses as far as he knew this fall was temporary and that soon, the market would be stable, and so would the stocks.

Rahul, who had good knowledge and skills and was into this business for the past 30 years couldn't withstand the present situation, he felt these 30 days had overpowered his 30 years of experience.

It's not that Rahul had not faced any such situations before, but this time, everything was different right from day one. He was losing control over himself and everything. happened against his beliefs and knowledge. In past situations, he always acknowledged the mistake and overcame it, either rectifying it by patiently waiting for the right time or just stopping right there and moving ahead, but this time, destiny had very cruel plans, and Rahul was sinking.

Feeling beaten down by money worries had adversely impacted his sleep, self-esteem, and energy levels. It had left him feeling, fearful, tense, and silent behaviour towards Mallvika and Neer, exacerbated pain and mood swings at peak, and even increased his depression and anxiety.

Rahul badly wanted to talk to Mallvika, but he repeatedly failed. His guilt of betrayal was not allowing him to talk to her. On the other hand, Mallvika, even though she believed Rahul's words, couldn't stop doubting his actions and behaviour, which pointed out a different scenario. Mallvika's heart was continuously fighting with her mind as her heart witnessed Rahul's loyalty, and her mind could see the trauma Rahul was going through. It was like there was a war between the trust and the doubts. Finally, her trust in Rahul overruled her doubts. Yet Mallvika continuously felt very restless and couldn't understand the reason for her anxiety.

Rahul's inner conscience spoke to him,

"Mallvika is my inner soul strength, "atma bala," Neer is my repletion, the family was my obligation, friends were my motivation, and business was my obsession. Destiny had already separated me from my family, my friends, and now my business, and all these I could sustain as my inner strength. Mallvika was always by my side. But by my acts, I have distanced myself from Mallvika and Neer, too; nothing is left. Even though my present loss will be compensated from the profit made from the recent trade and the savings and investment will be undisturbed, the guilt of betraying Mallvika and the insecurity of me not getting indulged in further trades is killing me." Rahul's thoughts had taken a diversion; he felt he had lost everything by betraying his beloved, and he was not worthy of any kind of apology.

The trade and fear of further trading had a traumatic effect on Rahul, was now scared of himself; he started believing that he had lost self-control and that, in the future, he would tend to indulge in more trade. The loss occurred now had not distributed any of his planned savings and capital, but any further loss in the future would ruin the lives of his loved ones; his actions could impact important life milestones, such as their retirement plan and paying for Neer's education. He felt that there was no coming back from the guilt and insecurities and, therefore, took actions that exacerbated the situation.

Experiencing such emotional difficulties is closely connected to the development and persistence of common mental disorders such as depression, self-harm behaviours, and higher suicide rates.

CHAPTER 24

Ultimate Destiny Plays its Role....

It was a Thursday morning, Rahul woke up early and got ready, he performed his daily Pooja and was waiting to go to the Jalaram temple. Mallvika had woken up late as it was Thursday, there was no breakfast to be made. Rahul and Mallvika sat down in the balcony, they had a general conversation but the duo's minds were occupied with several thoughts. Rahul was still gathering courage to tell Mallvika about the trade and the loss.

Mallvika was feeling helpless as she couldn't find any solution to the problem Rahul was going through, she was not even aware of the actual matter. She chose to be by his side all the time to make sure he feels her availability and on the contrary Mallvika's presence made Rahul feel more guilty as he couldn't face her.

The lovebirds always understood each other's silence, but today, they were clueless about what exactly was happening.

There was a call from Keyur to proceed to the temple. Rahul was ready he said, "Mallu hu jau chu" and left, Mallvika as always escorted Rahul till the entrance and then from the balcony, Rahul also looked up to convey goodbye.

As per routine, Rahul Keyur and Nipul first went to the temple and then to their favourite restaurant for breakfast. During the breakfast, they spoke about the two-day later weekend trip that the BONDS were going to celebrate friendship day. As they were done with breakfast, Rahul collected food packs for AANADANAM that he gave to the needy on his way back.

Rahul reached home. There was some time for the market to start, so he sat with Mallvika, who was having her breakfast. There were few conversations regarding the arrival of Jasumati, who was landing in Chennai today as Mallvika and Jasumati were travelling to the UK five days later.

It was time for the market to open, so Rahul moved toward the workspace and soon got involved in trading. It was a busy day for Rahul due to the violation in the market. Rahul was not sure what he wanted to do with the stocks he was holding on to as his stocks had not shown much a moment.

Rahul completed his after-market work. The duo and Jasumati had lunch together; Rahul and Jasumati had a few conversations regarding her health.

Rahul left for Keyur's art gallery after he completed his clients' accounts and lunch. At the gallery he had a few good moments with Keyur and then finished his gallery related work. He then left for home as he was feeling a bit restless about his stock position and yet couldn't take any decision.

Rahul was back home early, Mallvika was a bit worried on his early arrival. She couldn't hold anymore and finally spoke to Rahul with a tone of request," Rahul what's the matter? You always deal with the client's pressure but this time you look totally broken. Are you scared of any defaulters, can you please tell me what is it? I can sense and feel you have something going on in your head."

Rahul had no words but replied with total calmness," Mallu, I just want to be alone for some time. Please leave me alone, and I will be fine." Mallvika decided to sit silently by his side as she was not ready to leave him alone. They sat for almost an hour without any kind of conversation, but Rahul felt a bit uncomfortable and got up to do some work; he said," Mallu, I need to complete a few client's accounts, and masi (Jasumati) is awake, so you continue with your work." Mallvika's heart was not allowing her to leave Rahul, but she had to, as it was tea time for Jasumati, so she left the room. Her constant attention was on Rahul. She kept coming to Rahul just to check if he was okay, and she found him busy accounting.

Neer went to Rahul before going for her workout, she spoke about her day and asked Rahul the same. Rahul asked Neer not to go to gym as she looked very tired but Neer preferred as that's the only physical activity she did.

Mallvika got free and proceeded back towards Rahul; on Mallvika's sudden entry, Rahul got ambushed as though he was caught red-handed, but soon he got normal. Mallvika was a bit astonished by his reaction, but she felt it was due to her unanticipated entry. She sat for a while, then Rahul insisted," Mallu, I am fine, and I think you should be with masi as she is all alone; it looks awkward, and don't worry, I am almost done and will come out in some time." Mallvika once again left the room unheartily as she wanted to spend every second with him.

Rahul was done with his work, and when he came out, Mallvika reminded him about going to Sai temple. Rahul replied," Mallu, I visited the Sai temple in the morning on my way back from Jalaram temple, and I feel too exhausted, so you carry on; I will not join." Mallvika knew he was giving excuses and was not okay with it, so she insisted he join. They both left for Sai darshan, and on the way back, Rahul packed his favourite idly. They were back home and started their dinner; Neer was just back from her workout, and she accompanied the family to the dinner table. Rahul asked Neer to eat, but she was exhausted and wanted to take a shower, so she shared a bit from Rahul and Mallvika's plate. There was a normal conversation for some time, and then Rahul went to bed.

Rahul was watching television while in bed, Mallvika once went to him to say good night, then she accompanied Jasumati. Neer also went to Rahul to see if he was fine. Rahul asked her to keep his phone on charging and switch off the lights. Neer wished him good night and left.

Mallvika asked Jasumati about her requirements for the UK, and then later, Mallvika shared her happiness "Mummy, with Sai's blessings, everything is good; Rahul has well planned all our future needs, and everything required for Neer is also kept aside, now when the appropriate time comes we just have to execute it well. All our wounds have been healed, and we have forgiven all that has happened in the past. Everything is so very sought, and I hope the life ahead is just like what we have planned. Just then, Rahul had come out to drink water and went back to his room.

After some time, Mallvika went to check on Rahul, and she found him sleeping; she felt a peace that he could sleep as it would give his mind relaxation from all the stress he had over the day.

Jasumati and Mallvika had a long conversation and later went to bed. Neer also, after chatting with her naniji (grandmother), went to her room to study. Mallvika wrapped all her work and went to sleep.

She sat beside and gazed at Rahul, who was sleeping. She so very much wanted to talk to Rahul as she had terribly missed him throughout the day, even though the duos were together most of the time. She lifted her hand to gently caress his hair but stopped midway as she realised her touch could disturb or break Rahul's sleep, and she couldn't make an effort to take that risk. She slept but was extremely missing the cuddling. Mallvika couldn't sleep for quite some time. Then, finally, she slept with the hopes of a better tomorrow.

Neer was also awake till 2:00 am, busy studying.

Finally, all were in a deep sleep, and suddenly, at 4:50 am, the doorbell rang incessantly; Mallvika could hear the first few

   Destiny and Karma: Hand in Hand

bells in her deep sleep, and then suddenly she woke up with a jerk and ran towards the door, as she opened she saw their apartment security guards were at the door screaming we think sir has fainted due to electric shock, please come soon. Mallvika initially couldn't understand what they said, but on repetition, she could grasp what they were screaming about; she instantly denied saying sir is at home. He is sleeping. The guards repeated themselves, and they sounded very sure; this made Mallvika's heart stop, and she ran to check, as she was not ready to believe them, she reached she found Rahul missing, and she stood dumbstruck. For a few seconds, there was no reaction, but soon, she gathered herself and ran towards Neer. She woke her up by stating the incident, and both ran in madness; as they reached the ground floor, they saw Rahul on the floor. Neer ran to check on his pulse, and Mallvika tried calling Rahul, but there was no response; Neer couldn't feel the pulse.....

Epilogue

FINAL KARMA.......

Thursday evening, I was just back home early; Mallu was so worried and concerned and tried talking to me regarding what was bothering me. I somehow avoided the conversation by asking her to leave me alone for some time. She understood my feelings and chose not to distribute me, but at the same time, her concern for me had not allowed her to leave me alone, so she sat beside me quietly.

My mind was constantly hunting for answers to the question, why am I not able to make a decision? Why is that I am losing control? What is that holding me? Why is it that I am not concentrating on solving it when I have the solution right before me? I have been in such a situation before and I have faced and solved it. Today also I have a solution to the problem, yet I am stuck, what is stopping me? What is different this time?

The loss I am facing today will be compensated by the profits I had made the past few weeks, so basically it is nullified, yet something is bothering eminently.

I feel I am losing control over my inner consciousness, the biggest proof is I have started hiding things from Mallu and this guilt is breaking me apart. At present too she is just sitting beside me for so long, unquestioningly and confidently believing in me and yet I am not telling her the truth. She trusts me blindly and I am proving her blind.

We are at a stage where we can relax and enjoy the rest of our lives. But my actions scare me. I think in the past few weeks, I have developed the habit of indulging in personal trading, and if I keep repeating these actions, I will ruin everything. I have no right to drag Mallu and Neer into this pit, and my unrestrained behaviour will definitely decimate everything. I can't allow any such things to happen to Mallu and Neer; I am at fault, I am guilty, and the punishment should be given to me and only me. I don't deserve to live anymore and to end this action of mine, I need to end myself; there is no other way. Yes, this is the right thing to save Mallu and Neer; if not, my addiction will end their lives, too, and I can't allow that to happen.

Is it my fate that is forcing me to do this? Is it a sign of destiny? Is this meant to happen?..

Mallu knows every detail of our savings, investments and banks but regarding my business and clients I need to write down and arrange it well so tomorrow everything could be managed at ease.

Rahul had filed all clients' and business-related papers on Mark.

I have to write a confession note so no one is blamed for my act...

DEAR MALLU AND NEER

I AM SORRY I AM TAKING THIS COWARDLY STEP AS I HAVE BETRAYED YOU PEOPLE; I HAVE NOT BEEN LOYAL TO YOU PEOPLE. IF I AM AROUND, I WILL BE A BIG LIABILITY TO YOU PEOPLE.SO TAKING THIS STEP HAS BECOME COMPULSORY. THE FINANCIAL LOSS TO ME IS LITTLE, BUT THE LOSS OF BETRAYING YOU PEOPLE IS KILLING ME. IN SPITE OF PROMISING YOU PEOPLE THAT I WILL NOT INDULGE IN SPECULATION, I DID.

OFF LATE, COMING BACK FROM TURKEY, I STARTED TRADING AND WAS LOSING AND GAINING REGULARLY, AND THIS BECAME A HABIT OF MINE. MY INTENTION WAS TO COVER WHAT I LOST RECENTLY.

AFTER COMING BACK FROM THE ANNIVERSARY, I WAS STUCK BADLY, AND I STARTED ADDING TO MY PROBLEMS, AND THINGS WENT OUT OF MY HAND.

I AM UNABLE TO SHOW MY FACE TO YOU BOTH; I AM SORRY.

I AM SORRY, MY FRIENDS. I AM SORRY, MY DEAR FAMILY MEMBERS.

MALLU, I HAVE BETRAYED YOU IN EVERY COUNT OF LIFE. PLEASE DO NOT FORGIVE ME AND HATE ME. I LOVE YOU, MALLU…. SORRY...

NEER, DON'T WORRY ABOUT YOUR FUTURE; I THINK ENOUGH IS THERE IN THE FORM OF SAVINGS IN VARIOUS FORMS FOR YOUR FUTURE. NEER, PLEASE TAKE CARE OF MUMMY. AND BE A SUCCESSFUL DOCTOR.

MESSAGE TO MY DEAR FRIENDS PLEASE TAKE CARE OF MALLU & NEER.

DEAR FAMILY MEMBERS, PLEASE TAKE CARE OF MALLU & NEER.

RIPUL & DHIRAJ, PLEASE HELP MALLU IN FINANCIAL ACTIVITY.

SORRY ALL OF YOU.....

PLEASE TAKE NOTE THAT I AM SOLELY RESPONSIBLE FOR THIS EXTREME STEP; I AM NOT BLAMING ANYBODY.

RAHUL

www.ingramcontent.com/pod-product-compliance
Lightning Source LLC
Chambersburg PA
CBHW051155130726
47988CB00005B/2129